Making Change Irresistible

Making Change
Irresistible

**Overcoming
Resistance
to Change
in Your
Organization**

Ken Hultman

DAVIES-BLACK PUBLISHING
Palo Alto, California

Published by Davies-Black Publishing, an imprint of Consulting Psychologists Press, Inc., 3803 East Bayshore Road, Palo Alto, CA 94303; 800-624-1765.

Special discounts on bulk quantities of Davies-Black books are available to corporations, professional associations, and other organizations. For details, contact the Director of Book Sales at Davies-Black Publishing, an imprint of Consulting Psychologists Press, Inc., 3803 East Bayshore Road, Palo Alto, CA 94303; 650-691-9123; Fax 650-988-0673.

02 01 00 99 98   10 9 8 7 6 5 4 3 2 1

Printed in the United States of America

Library of Congress Cataloging-in-Publication Data

Hultman, Ken.
  Making change irresistible : overcoming resistance to change in your
  organization / Ken Hultman.
      p.   cm.
  Includes biographical references and index.
  ISBN 0-89106-121-5
  1. Organizational change. 2. Organizational behavior. I. Title.
HD58.8.H838   1998

658.4'063—dc21   98-18575
                                                                             CIP

FIRST EDITION

First printing 1998

This book is dedicated to
the memories of my father,
Kenneth Elmer Hultman,
and
my father-in-law,
Leo Glenn Fradenburg, Ph.D.,
both of whom I loved dearly

Contents

About the Author   ix

Preface   xi

Understanding Human Behavior and Change

1   So You Want to Make Some Changes?   3

2   Understanding Human Behavior   15

3   The Motivational Cycle   35

4   The Dynamics of Change   51

5   Changes in Organizational Reality   65

2

Diagnosing and Overcoming Resistance to Change

6   Assessing Resistance   95

7   Locating Causes of Resistance   109

8   Diagnosing Causes of Resistance   139

9   Building Trust   151

10   Strategies for Overcoming Resistance   171

Appendix: Adapting to a Changing
          Health Care Environment
          Jon Hultman, DPM, MBA   195

Notes   201

Bibliography   203

Index   207

About the Author

Ken Hultman received his B.S. degree in sociology and his M.A. degree in counseling from Arizona State University, and his Ed.D. degree in counseling psychology from Rutgers University, with a major in group process. He taught graduate courses in counseling at Florida State University for $1^1/_2$ years and was a staff psychologist at a community mental health clinic for one year before shifting his focus to human resource development in 1974.

Hultman served as director of staff development at the Texas Rehabilitation Commission from 1976 to 1979. During that time, he provided the leadership necessary for the training department to make the transition from an administrative to a professional human resource development department. After *The Path of Least Resistance: Preparing Employees for Change* was published, Ken took a position as a training consultant with Development Dimensions International. Over the next six years, he trained people from more than a hundred Fortune 500 companies in the implementation of supervisory and management training programs and personnel selection systems. He has also published articles on managing change, training program implementation, training techniques, behavior modeling learning technology, and performance motivation.

A program designed by Hultman, *Preparing Yourself for Change,* has been used at General Electric as part of their leadership and empowerment process, and material he has written on performance motivation is included in the Internal Organizational Development Curriculum at General Motors. His workbook, *The Performance Tune-Up Kit: A Guide to Career*

Planning, is used by organizations in the United States and other countries. Hultman is certified as a training consultant by the International Board of Certified Trainers, Inc. Ken is vice president for organizational development at Menno Haven, Inc., in Chambersburg, Pennsylvania.

You can write to the author at 1117 Fiddler's Road, Chambersburg, PA 17201.

Preface

Action and reaction, ebb and flow, trial and error, change—this is the rhythm of living. Out of our over-confidence, fear; out of our fear, clearer vision, fresh hope. And out of hope—progress.

—Bruce Barton

John Kotter defines leadership as bringing about constructive change, which is accomplished by developing a vision, aligning people to that vision, and motivating people to move toward the vision. The failure of organizational change efforts usually is due not to a lack of vision or good ideas, but to resistance from those whose support is necessary to fulfill the vision.

Visionaries tend to have a bias toward change that is not shared by many others. Regardless of how good a change may be, a certain amount of resistance is almost always inevitable. Thus, as the human drama plays itself out each day in organizations, a creative tension develops between those championing change and those seeking stability. Resistance to change can range from minor to explosive. If not dealt with properly, of course, minor resistance can become major, and even a small amount of resistance takes time and energy from more productive pursuits. It is an unnecessary detour on the road to the future.

Some resistance to change is obvious and can be dealt with swiftly, but more often than not it is subtle. People attempt to maneuver around change without being detected because they have a powerful will to survive. When they feel threatened by change, whether the threat is real or imagined, they look for ways to prevent it, frustrating those endeavoring to move their organizations forward in the midst of chaos and uncertainty.

This book is intended to serve as a strategic and tactical manual for battling resistance to organizational change. It is written for anyone who has a role in leading others through change—executives, managers, supervisors, human resource professionals, and internal and external organization development (OD) consultants. The word *irresistible* in the title points to two challenges. The first is to present change in such a way that people are enticed and intrigued by it. This isn't always possible, of course, so the second challenge is to minimize or lower resistance. Since your ultimate success depends on how well you manage change, a thorough understanding of how to handle resistance is essential.

Many books about organizational change touch on the subject of resistance, but they tend to deal with it in a cursory fashion or make it appear simple to resolve. The truth is that most resistance is tough to diagnose and even tougher to overcome. My goal is to provide a comprehensive treatment of the subject, addressing a multitude of issues encountered by organizational leaders.

Since 1972 I have worked as a therapist, a staff manager, a line manager, a business owner, a university professor, an internal consultant, and an external consultant. I have done individual, marriage, family, and group counseling; offered executive coaching; given workshops and seminars on personal and career growth, supervision and management, interviewing skills, team building, performance improvement, managing change, and conflict resolution; and provided OD consulting with organizations as small as family farms and as large as Fortune 500 companies.

What these diverse activities had in common is that they all had to do with fostering change—personal, interpersonal, or organizational. By listening intently to people and nudging them toward change, I have encountered more forms of resistance than I can count. I have also experimented with a multitude of approaches to overcoming resistance. No two situations have been exactly the same, so I have found this work both challenging and fulfilling. Working with resistance for so long and in so many ways has refined my understanding of this subject. Everything I have learned about how to diagnose and overcome resistance for the past three decades is contained in these pages. I am happy to be able to pass the knowledge along to you.

The book represents a revision of my earlier work, *The Path of Least Resistance: Preparing Employees for Change,* published in 1979. In the years since then, I have expanded the concepts as I have gained additional experience in counseling, coaching, training and consulting. I have retained about 20 percent of the original material and added a substantial amount of new information. While this book focuses on change and resistance in organizational settings, it deals with human behavior in general, and I encourage you to apply the ideas to your personal life.

The material is organized into two parts. Part 1 discusses the key concepts I have found essential to understanding human behavior and change: needs, facts, beliefs, feelings, values, and actions. Taken together, these concepts comprise what I call the *motivational cycle,* which explains why people choose either to change or to resist. Building on the concepts presented in Part 1, Part 2 takes a detailed look at how to diagnose resistance using the Resistance Matrix and how to overcome resistance using the Resistance Strategy Model. Four nonstandardized inventories and a variety of practical exercises are included to augment your own learning, as well as the learning of those you work with as a manager, trainer, or consultant.

I would like to thank the people who helped me with this project. Mike Morris, president of the Contact Group, Inc., in Pittsburgh, gave me opportunities to work with him on many challenging training and consulting assignments. The mentoring I received from Mike stretched my thinking and planted the seeds for many of the ideas presented in this volume. Linda Robinson, a superb instructional technologist with the Contact Group, helped me clarify some of my abstract notions and make them more concrete. I'm also very grateful to the Davies-Black team that embraced this project with such enthusiasm, providing me with a thoroughly enjoyable publishing experience: to Melinda Adams Merino, whose suggestions allowed me to make the book more practical by improving its organization; to Laura Simonds, whose marketing expertise, energy, and patience guided me through the parts of this venture I understood the least; and to Jill L. Anderson-Wilson, whose attention to detail allowed us to breeze through the production process. Finally, I'd like to thank my wife, Pat, who encouraged me to stick with the project when it became tedious and frustrating. She also provided me with invaluable help by proofreading the manuscript each time I made a substantial change.

KENNETH E. HULTMAN

Understanding Human Behavior and Change

I have always wondered what makes people tick. Why do they do what they do? My early attempts to understand myself led to a keen interest in the social and behavioral sciences in college and graduate school. That interest has continued unabated during my thirty years as a therapist and organizational development specialist.

I have seen many people attempt to implement organizational change without trying to understand the people affected by it. Some of them looked upon this as a nuisance or as a necessary evil. In either case the results were usually frustrating and sometimes even disastrous. In contrast, I've seen others take the time to understand people and then reap the benefits by being able to implement change successfully.

Part 1 is intended to help you deepen your understanding of human behavior and the change process so you can become more effective in planning and implementing change. Chapter 1, So You Want to Make Some Changes?, describes eight conditions under which people will support change and includes the Change Opinion Survey, which can help you diagnose resistance to organizational change.

Chapter 2, Understanding Human Behavior, discusses five psychological needs that an organization must meet to promote high morale and productivity. People tend to be more supportive of change in organizations that pay attention to their psychological needs and to resist change in organizations that neglect these needs. The Psychological Need Fulfillment Inventory is included to help you identify unmet psychological needs that could be causing resistance to change.

Chapter 3, The Motivational Cycle, presents what I consider to be the key concepts for understanding why people do what they do: facts, beliefs, values, and behavior. You will become adept at identifying these concepts, which will serve you well as you plan and implement change. Chapter 4, The Dynamics of Change, discusses the process of change and explains the roles of facts, beliefs, values, and behavior in the psychology of change.

Basic facts about the world of work have changed, and many beliefs, values, and behaviors that were useful in the past are now antithetical to those necessary for success in the global marketplace. Chapter 5, Changes in Organizational Reality, compares and contrasts these beliefs, values, and behaviors and describes in detail eight values highly prized by progressive organizations. The chapter includes the Megavalue Scale to help you assess the extent to which people currently embrace those eight values, and the Plan for Personal Change, which prepares you to help people move toward more viable beliefs, values, and behaviors.

1

So You Want to Make Some Changes?

Biochemist Dr. Bill Jenson, president of a large medical technology firm, knew that his business wouldn't survive unless he made some radical changes. He and five other scientists had started the business in his basement fifteen years earlier with a thousand dollars and five new patents. In fifteen years their investment had grown into a two-billion-dollar enterprise, consisting of twenty-five thousand employees at five plant sites within a fifty-mile radius. Starting out in disposable medical supplies, they expanded to precision instruments and then into the fields of genetics and bioengineering. Bill was always telling people that the heavens couldn't compare to the miniature universe revealed by one of his company's sophisticated electron microscopes.

Disposable supplies had been the company's bread and butter for a long time, but patents on these products would expire in two years. The firm's research in genetics and bioengineering was on the cutting edge—they were several years ahead of the competition—but it would be years before the new patents would have a positive effect on the bottom line. Meanwhile, the expected onslaught of competition in the disposable sector would mean a sharp drop in market share, even if prices were cut, as they inevitably would be. Since this part of the business accounted for 50 percent of the total earnings, immediate action was required to protect the company's financial position until its research initiatives paid off.

Ten thousand semiskilled employees worked in the manufacturing division producing disposable medical supplies. Bill wanted to avoid downsizing because the cost of training every employee was about five thousand dollars, and it took about a year to bring a new employee up to peak productivity. In addition, because of the nature of its work, the company had many trade secrets and a complex set of safety procedures to control infection and prevent contamination. Employees who were committed to the organization and abided by the safety guidelines were therefore regarded as valuable intellectual capital. In the long run, it would be more cost-effective to upgrade the skills of these employees so they could work in precision instruments, genetics, and bioengineering than it would be to downsize and hire people from the outside.

Bill had these thoughts on his mind as he arrived for the Capital Area CEO Roundtable, an annual meeting for entrepreneurs on the latest thinking in organizational leadership. After attending a session entitled "How to Create a Learning Organization," Bill was very excited because he saw immediate application to his issues. His company had always emphasized training, but most of the budget for people in research and development, marketing, and human resources was spent on conferences. Bill had always questioned the benefit of this type of training for the organization.

Bill knew that after completing the mandatory job-skills course, manufacturing employees took little initiative to receive additional training. Since most of them had no formal education beyond high school, and the wage scale was quite high for people with that amount of education, very few of them showed interest in career advancement. For these reasons, the idea of creating a work environment where employees took responsibility for their own learning and developed a learning contract relating the development of knowledge and skills to organizational needs struck a responsive chord with Bill.

Upon his return home, Bill enthusiastically sent a memo to employees describing his plans to change their use of the training budget and inviting them to attend a workshop on the learning organization concept. Much to Bill's surprise, the reaction to his memo was swift and uniformly negative. Bill spent the next several days listening to a wide range of employee objections to his ideas. Frustrated by his inability to persuade people that the new program would benefit both them and the company, and baffled by their resistance, Bill sat in his office pondering what to do next.

Gaining Support for Change

Support for change, of course, is the opposite of resistance. In any given situation, there are eight reasons why people will support change:

▲ **They believe their needs are not being met currently.** In other words, they are dissatisfied with the status quo. They either don't believe they're getting ahead or they believe they're going backward.

▲ **They believe the change will make it easier for them to meet their eeeds.** They believe it will eliminate unnecessary, tedious, or unpleasant work.

▲ **They believe the benefits outweigh the risks.** They expect that it will result in some personal gain. They expect a new challenge or opportunity as a result. They believe the risks are worth taking.

▲ **They believe the change is necessary to avoid or escape a harmful situation.** Some examples would be bankruptcy, a hostile takeover, or a decline in market share, profit, revenue, productivity, quality, morale, competitive position, and so on.

▲ **They believe the change process is being handled properly.** They believe they are being treated fairly. They trust those responsible for the change. They are being given an opportunity to provide input into the change. People should be asked for input if

they will be affected by the change
you need their commitment to implement the change
they have information or ideas to contribute
they expect to be involved
they could learn from the experience
you want to expand or strengthen your base of support

▲ **They believe the change will work.** They believe it is the right time for the change. They believe adequate resources (staff, time, money, equipment, etc.) have been allocated to the change effort.

▲ **The change is consistent with their values.** People will support change if it's consistent with their standards or represents something they believe is important.

▲ **They believe those responsible for the change can be trusted.** Even if people don't completely agree with a change, they're more likely to go along with it if they trust those responsible for it. People tend to have confidence in those they trust, and they tend to be suspicious of those they don't trust.

Returning to our example, after pondering the matter further, Bill decided to give the Change Opinion Survey to a sample of faculty and administration. This instrument, which you will find on pages 9–12, assesses eight common causes of resistance to change. The results that Bill obtained are presented on the Change Opinion Profile on page 7 (because of their similarities, results from research and development, marketing, and human resources were combined for reporting purposes).

While almost everyone felt that the change process was handled improperly, Bill noticed some differences among the departments. Manufacturing said that the change wouldn't necessarily keep something bad from happening, while research and development, marketing, and human resources indicated that their needs were being met already; that is, they saw no reason to change.

After pondering the results, Bill familiarized himself with the eight common causes of resistance described in Chapter 8 and the methods for overcoming resistance presented in Chapters 9 and 10. Then he began to develop his strategy for dealing with the situation. He knew that he would have to apologize to everyone for not involving them sooner, as he normally would have done, but he also knew that he couldn't use the same approach to overcome resistance in all the departments.

After gathering additional information, Bill discovered that, even though it was never meant to be this way, many people in research and development, marketing, and human resources saw attending conferences as a perk, and they often built their vacation plans around these meetings. They therefore saw the change as something that would take this perk away. Bill met with people from these departments separately, clarifying the purpose of the training budget and stressing the need for the company to receive a greater return on investment from employee participation in training. Although most of them still didn't like the change, they could see Bill's rationale and agreed to support the move to a learning organization.

Since manufacturing didn't believe the change was needed to keep something bad from happening in the future, Bill took a different approach. Upon reflection, he realized that he had not given them enough information about the expected decline in disposable medical supply sales. In a series of meetings at all five plants, he told them that the company wanted to keep them as employees, but for this to happen they needed to take more responsibility for developing skills in areas where expansion was anticipated. Once these employees understood the seriousness of the situation, they began to see a greater need for a learning organization. While they ~~and~~ had concerns about their ability to acquire the skills required to work in the areas of precision instruments, genetics, and bioengineering, Bill assured them that he would provide the resources needed for them to make this transition. Seeing that Bill was trying to help them prepare for the company's future, which would be very different from the past, they agreed to support his new program.

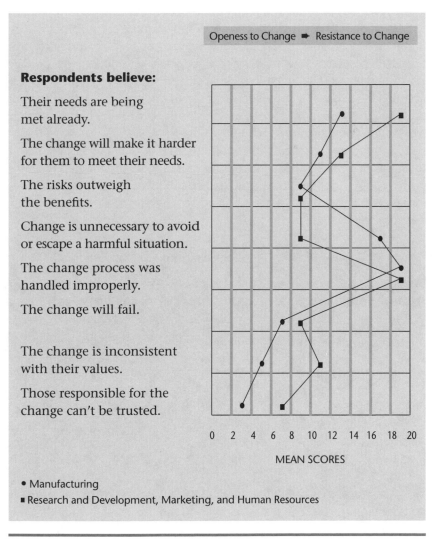

Respondents believe:

Their needs are being met already.

The change will make it harder for them to meet their needs.

The risks outweigh the benefits.

Change is unnecessary to avoid or escape a harmful situation.

The change process was handled improperly.

The change will fail.

The change is inconsistent with their values.

Those responsible for the change can't be trusted.

Openess to Change ➡ Resistance to Change

MEAN SCORES

• Manufacturing

■ Research and Development, Marketing, and Human Resources

Figure 1   Change Opinion Profile

How to Use This Book

A survey of Fortune 500 executives concluded that resistance is the main reason organizational changes fail.[1] No matter how good change may be for organizations, it still has to be implemented in an environment that includes people. It often takes strong, determined leadership, like that provided by Bill, to implement the kind of change that represents a radical departure from the past. Regardless of how large or small a change may be, however, expect resistance. With the rapid pace of technological advancement and the explosion of new information, organizational leaders today face special challenges as they try to gain support for change. A few quick pointers on how to implement change simply won't do. To be effective at promoting change, you need in-depth knowledge of the causes of resistance, as well as a wide range of skills to overcome resistance. This book offers concepts and tools that will enable you to acquire such knowledge and skills.

The book is intended for anyone whose job it is to lead others through change: executives, managers and supervisors, human resource professionals, and internal and external OD consultants. Content, instruments, and exercises are included to address the following specific learning needs:

Learning Need	Content
Understanding human behavior	Chapters 2–5
Personal growth	Chapters 2–5, Megavalue Scale, Plan for Personal Change
Team building	Chapter 2, Psychological Need Fulfillment Inventory; Chapter 9, Building Team Trust Workshop
Diagnosing resistance to change	Chapter 1, Change Opinion Survey; Chapter 2, Psychological Need Fulfillment Inventory; Chapter 6, Current/Desired Beliefs, Values and Behaviors Exercise; Chapter 7, Resistance Identification Exercise; Chapter 8, Resistance Diagnosis Exercise
Overcoming resistance to change	Chapter 9, Building Trust Exercise; Chapter 10, Plan of Action for Overcoming Resistance to Change

The Change Opinion Survey

Purpose

There are many possible causes of resistance to organizational change. I have identified the eight most common causes. Use the Change Opinion Survey to help determine if one or more of these eight common causes are responsible for resistance to a particular change. You will find a discussion of the eight common causes in Chapter 8.

Procedure

Administer the Change Opinion Survey prior to implementing change in order to prevent resistance or after resistance surfaces in order to minimize its impact. You can also administer it before and after a change as a way of evaluating the implementation.

The instrument can be given to everyone involved with a change or to a representative sample. An individual can also complete the instrument in order to understand more fully his or her reasons for resisting change. Specify the particular change being surveyed on the cover page of the instrument.

One way to use the data is to meet with those leading the change effort, display the completed Change Opinion Profile, and then facilitate a discussion of the reasons for resistance. Mean scores can range from 0 to 20. The higher a mean score, the more indication that a common cause is a reason for resistance. Mean scores above 14 indicate considerable resistance.

Following the discussion of causes, you can develop strategies for overcoming resistance. Some suggested strategies are presented in Chapters 9 and 10.

Directions

Read each item on the next two pages and circle the response that best describes your opinion. The scale is a continuum from 0 to 4, with 0 meaning strongly disagree and 4 meaning strongly agree. Your responses will be combined with others in the organization and will be kept confidential. You will receive a summary of the results once they have been compiled.

	Strongly Disagree ➡ Strongly Agree				
1. There isn't any need for the change.	0	1	2	3	4
2. The change makes it harder to get our work done.	0	1	2	3	4
3. The risks of the change outweigh the benefits.	0	1	2	3	4
4. We can remain competitive without changing.	0	1	2	3	4
5. I didn't have any input into the change.	0	1	2	3	4
6. The change isn't going to work.	0	1	2	3	4
7. The change emphasizes the wrong priorities.	0	1	2	3	4
8. No one is telling us the real reason for the change.	0	1	2	3	4
9. We seem to change for the sake of change.	0	1	2	3	4
10. The change will lower productivity.	0	1	2	3	4
11. The change will have negative long-range consequences.	0	1	2	3	4
12. We're just jumping on the bandwagon with other organizations.	0	1	2	3	4
13. The timing of the change is bad.	0	1	2	3	4
14. The change sounds good in theory but not in reality.	0	1	2	3	4
15. The change will take us in the wrong direction.	0	1	2	3	4
16. Management isn't being honest with us about the change.	0	1	2	3	4
17. People are going along with the change, but they don't agree with it.	0	1	2	3	4
18. The change will lower morale.	0	1	2	3	4
19. The change will do more harm than good.	0	1	2	3	4
20. Nothing bad will happen if we don't change.	0	1	2	3	4

	Strongly Disagree ➡ Strongly Agree				
21. Nobody cares what I think about the change.	0	1	2	3	4
22. We lack the resources necessary to implement the change successfully.	0	1	2	3	4
23. The change isn't important to me.	0	1	2	3	4
24. Those responsible for the change have a hidden agenda.	0	1	2	3	4
25. I don't understand the reasons for the change.	0	1	2	3	4
26. The change creates more hurdles to jump over.	0	1	2	3	4
27. I don't see anything good coming from this change.	0	1	2	3	4
28. Management is using scare tactics to get us to accept the change.	0	1	2	3	4
29. Management asked for our ideas but then didn't use them.	0	1	2	3	4
30. We've tried changes like this before and they didn't work.	0	1	2	3	4
31. The change doesn't relate to my values.	0	1	2	3	4
32. Information about the change is being withheld from us.	0	1	2	3	4
33. Most people can't see what the change will accomplish.	0	1	2	3	4
34. The change adds to our workload.	0	1	2	3	4
35. The change is bad for business.	0	1	2	3	4
36. We can grow as an organization without the change.	0	1	2	3	4
37. The change is being implemented too quickly.	0	1	2	3	4
38. The change will last for a while, then we'll go back to the old way.	0	1	2	3	4
39. The change is distracting us from more important issues.	0	1	2	3	4
40. I don't trust the people making the change.	0	1	2	3	4

Calculating Scores

This instrument consists of forty items, five pertaining to each of the eight common causes of resistance. You can develop a Change Opinion Profile by following these procedures:

1. Total the scores of each person completing the instrument for the eight causes. Items pertaining to each reason are:

   They believe their needs are being met already: 1, 9, 17, 25, 33

   They believe the change will make it harder for them to meet their needs: 2, 10, 18, 26, 34

   They believe the risks outweigh the benefits: 3, 11, 19, 27, 35

   They believe change is unnecessary to avoid or escape a harmful situation: 4, 12, 20, 28, 36

   They believe the change process is being handled improperly: 5, 13, 21, 29, 37

   They believe the change will fail: 6, 14, 22, 30, 38

   The change is inconsistent with their values: 7, 15, 23, 31, 39

   They believe those responsible for the change can't be trusted: 8, 16, 24, 32, 40

2. Add the totals of all respondents together for each common cause and divide these totals by the number of respondents completing the instrument. This will give you the mean or average scores for this group of respondents.

3. Place a dot at the corresponding point on the profile for the eight causes, and connect the dots with a line.

Change Opinion Profile

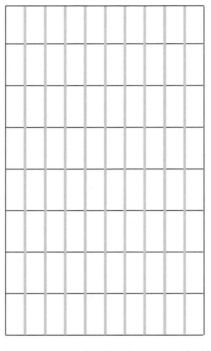

Openess to Change ➡ Resistance to Change

Respondents believe:

Their needs are being met already.

The change will make it harder for them to meet their needs.

The risks outweigh the benefits.

Change is unnecessary to avoid or escape a harmful situation.

The change process is being handled improperly.

The change will fail.

The change is inconsistent with their values.

Those responsible for the change can't be trusted.

0 2 4 6 8 10 12 14 16 18 20

MEAN SCORES

Understanding
Human Behavior

It is impossible to understand the dynamics of change and people's resistance to change without knowing something about motivation. Why do people do anything at all? What we can assert with some confidence is this: all behavior is purposeful, ar.d the purpose is to meet needs. An organization can be defined, therefore, as a group of people working together to meet needs. The most effective way to gain insight into human behavior is to ask, "What need are these people trying to meet?"

Needs are experienced as urges and desires originating from within us. An unfulfilled need is accompanied by pain, which can be physical, emotional, psychological, or spiritual, depending on the need. Fulfilling a need, in contrast, produces either pleasure or relief from pain. People are not islands unto themselves, capable of meeting their needs in isolation from others; the process of meeting needs requires them to interact with the world and with other people.

Trying to get our needs met is risky. When we want something we face a predicament, because there's always the possibility that we won't be able to get it. The future is always uncertain, and no matter how carefully we plan, we are vulnerable to having bad things happen. Acting on needs within a context of vulnerability is part of our human reality. Since our vulnerability is constant and we're aware of it either consciously or subconsciously before we act, our awareness produces anxiety and fear. Most of us regard this as normal until the level of perceived risk intensifies. Thus, in addition to desire, fear is a powerful motivator.

In the struggle to get our needs met, desire and fear walk hand in hand, and one is always capable of overpowering the other.

In any situation there are four courses of action open to us. We can

▲ **Escape** something we perceive is dangerous
▲ **Avoid** something we perceive is dangerous
▲ **Attack** something we perceive is dangerous
▲ **Pursue** something we believe is important

Escaping, avoiding, and attacking are primarily defensive, self-protective courses of action. Perceiving something or someone as dangerous evokes fear, triggering the well-known fight-or-flight response. Escaping and avoiding are flight responses, and attacking is a fight response. In situations where a real danger exists, such responses are often very appropriate and may even be necessary for survival. There are many times, however, when escaping, avoiding, and attacking are counterproductive. People often escape situations they should face, avoid opportunities that could help them learn, and attack people with whom they should be building alliances. While escaping, avoiding, and attacking may allow us to deal with an immediate danger, which is their purpose, they do nothing to help us make something positive happen in our lives. Also, these responses do nothing to eliminate our basic vulnerability as human beings. After the danger has passed, we still have to face anxiety and take risks if we intend to get our needs met.

Another problem is that our nervous system can't distinguish between real and imagined danger; under both sets of circumstances it reacts with fear. The perception of danger therefore will make us afraid, even if there's nothing to be afraid of. We are also capable of overreacting to real danger, making mountains out of molehills. I work with people in organizations who are afraid to give presentations to others. When I ask why, they often say that they worry about making fools of themselves. Sometimes the anxiety is so intense that they literally can't say anything; they choke on their words. I challenge them to reevaluate the danger and put it into a more realistic perspective. I also point out that this type of anxiety will keep them from achieving their career potential, and I challenge them to overcome it. If they're willing to try, I then take them through some exercises designed to desensitize the anxiety. Perceived danger, both real and imagined, not only inhibits people's performance but also is one of the primary reasons for resistance to change.

Of the four courses of action available to us, only pursuing is proactive and nondefensive, because it focuses on making good things happen, not on preventing bad things from happening. Pursuing is related to the concept of *empowerment,* because it means facing our vulnerability as human beings and taking the risks necessary to achieve our goals. Only by pursuing can we successfully meet our needs while doing what we believe is important in life. As we weigh our options in any situation, therefore, we must answer this question: Am I going to live my future or let fear live it for me?

According to Abraham Maslow, needs exist in a hierarchy of relative pre-potency, with physiological needs at the bottom, followed in order by safety, social, psychological, and self-actualization needs. He maintains that once people's lower-level needs are met, they focus on their higher-level needs. Since physiological and safety needs require no explanation, I will focus on the powerful but more subtle influence of social, psychological, and self-actualization needs of people in the workplace.

My formulation is different from the one put forth by Maslow in that I view social, psychological, and self-actualization needs as serving the overall purpose of allowing people to view themselves and be viewed by others as having worth and value as a person—the mega-goal of personality. Social psychologist William McDougal referred to self-worth as "the master sentiment." Many other psychologists have discussed the centrality of our need to maintain and enhance our self-worth. To perceive oneself as being worthwhile as a person instills one with a feeling of hope, whereas to perceive oneself as lacking worth creates a feeling of despair. When people feel bad about themselves it's hard to get them to do anything. If you're interested in motivating people, the single most effective approach is to help them have a more positive self-image.

Everything we do reflects on our worth in one way or another. We are always motivated to validate our worth, but since we can never be sure what's going to happen next, we're also vulnerable to having our sense of worth weakened. Therefore, although the need to feel worthy can propel us forward, fear of unworthiness can hold us back.

Because having a sense of worth is our central need, other social, psychological, and self-actualization needs serve as means to this end. We strive for a sense of worth through what psychologists have called the "drive for greatness," which focuses on competence, and the "drive for goodness," which focuses on integrity or ethics. To feel worthy, people must believe that they are both competent and ethical. Competence and integrity have both a personal and a social dimension, allowing us to distinguish four subneeds that serve the overall purpose of helping us validate our worth as human beings: mastery, a sense of meaning and

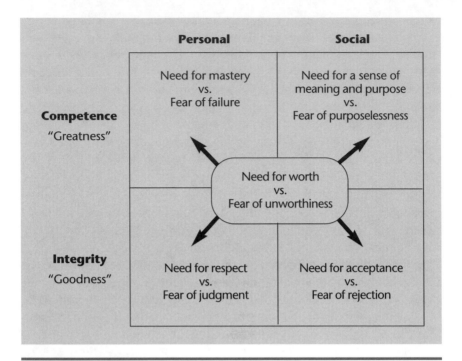

Figure 2   Psychological Needs

purpose, respect, and acceptance. In my experience, these are the needs most responsible for people's behavior in organizations. Although all four needs assert themselves more or less simultaneously, at any moment one will usually be more salient than the others. These needs are displayed graphically in Figure 2.

Mastery (Personal Competence)

People need to view themselves and be viewed by others as being competent and capable. This is what David McClelland refers to as the need for achievement. Frederick Herzberg lists achievement, responsibility, advancement, and the work itself as four of his five job satisfiers, all of which are indicators of one's competence. Mastery is personal in focus because the emphasis is on what we're capable of doing. The perception of being competent produces feelings of self-confidence and pride, increasing one's sense of worth, while the perception of being incompetent produces feelings of self-doubt and shame, lowering one's sense of worth. Although people have a need for mastery, they are also motivated by the fear of failure, which can cause them to avoid or escape situations where they anticipate poor performance. This can keep them from taking the risks necessary to develop and use their talents and abilities.

People in organizations want to view themselves and be viewed by others as competent, and yet I have been struck by how quick people are to judge each other incompetent. Although they rarely disclose their thoughts about this to each other, when they meet with me privately they make statements like these:

"They should never have selected him for that job."

"His incompetence is dragging all of us down."

"If they were hiring people based on merit, she never would have gotten that job."

"I don't know why they promoted him. There are many others around here more qualified."

When facilitating team building, I deliberately bring the issue of competence out in the open so it can be discussed directly, because people's confidence in each other's ability is often a key to developing cohesiveness. My goal is to move team members from judging each other to offering the support and encouragement that would make the team more effective. Teams perform better when members strive to help each other increase their competence.

A Sense of Meaning and Purpose (Social Competence)

People need to view themselves and be viewed by others as making a contribution to the team/organization. People not only need to feel that they've done a good job, but also to feel that their work is important. Herzberg lists recognition for achievement as his fifth job satisfier, because recognition is an indication that one's work is purposeful. Other writers refer to this as pride of accomplishment. A sense of meaning and purpose is social in emphasis, because it has to do with people's desire to leave the organization better off than it was when they arrived. This need, more than any other, addresses the question, "Why am I here?" The perception of making a contribution produces feelings of well-being and fulfillment, enhancing one's sense of worth, while the perception of not making a contribution brings feelings of depression, emptiness, and discouragement, lowering one's sense of worth. Although people have a need for a sense of meaning and purpose, they can also be motivated by a fear that their work will be insignificant, leading them to either search compulsively for ways of making a more important contribution or give in to a sense of uselessness and futility.

When I meet with organizational leaders one-on-one, they often let their guard down and reveal a deep sense of discouragement with their efforts. It's rare for anyone in the organization to ask them about their feelings, so they take advantage of the opportunity to open up with me. Painfully, they reveal such thoughts as these:

"I had such high expectations when I came here, but all I've done is put out one fire after the next."

"I can't think of one thing I've done that has made a bit of difference."

"Every idea I propose gets shot down."

"I've had nothing but one disappointment after the next. I'm not sure how much more of this I can take."

People who make such statements are really saying that they have lost their sense of purpose. To a large extent, their future effectiveness depends on their ability to regain this.

Respect (Personal Integrity)

People need to view themselves (self-respect) and be viewed by others as being ethical and honest. Maslow includes respect as one of our ego needs. Other writers talk about our need for dignity. Respect is personal in focus because the emphasis is on one's character, which speaks to the question, "What kind of a person am I?" The perception of being regarded as someone with high ethical standards produces a feeling of inner peace, increasing one's sense of worth; whereas the perception of being regarded as someone with low ethical standards is a threat to one's sense of worth. Although people have a need for respect, they can also be motivated by a fear of being judged, causing them to become manipulative, defensively justify their actions, or engage in blame shifting.

In addition to judging others' competence, people are quick to judge each other's character. In one-on-one meetings, people often make comments like the following:

"I always take what he says with a grain of salt."

"People warned me about her the day I was hired."

"We get along fine, but I wouldn't turn my back on him."

It's interesting to note that people who aren't trusted almost always perceive themselves as being worthy of trust. During one-on-one performance feedback sessions, when I tell people that others don't trust them, they're often shocked and react defensively, saying such things as, "I've never done anything to hurt them," or, "Give me one example of a time when I was dishonest." The problem with trust issues is that people seldom bring them to the surface and deal with them directly. Unresolved concerns can lie dormant for years, subtly affecting people's behavior toward each other, even if there's no evidence to support the mistrust. When I facilitate team building, getting people to face these issues is high on my agenda because I know they won't be able to accomplish much unless they trust each other. I consider trust so important to understanding change and resistance to change that Chapter 9 is devoted entirely to this subject.

Acceptance (Social Integrity)

People need to view themselves and be viewed by others as being worthy of acceptance. McClelland refers to this as the need for affiliation, and Maslow calls it the need for belonging. Acceptance focuses on ethics, because people usually believe including others is right and that excluding them is wrong. People can be members of a team in a formal sense but still not feel like they've been accepted by others. There are many reasons why people can feel rejected, including their physical appearance, personality, race, religion, socioeconomic status, seniority, values, or beliefs. The perception of being accepted produces feelings of joy, happiness, and contentment, adding to one's sense of self-worth, while the perception of being rejected produces feelings of hurt, lowering one's sense of self-worth. Although people have a need for acceptance, they can also be motivated by a fear of rejection, causing them to either hold back from others or to become angry and lash out.

People become very discouraged when they don't feel accepted by others in an organization. This discouragement is revealed in such statements as the following:

"They ignore you unless you're a member of the 'good-old-boy' club."

"The discrimination is very subtle, but I feel it all the time."

"They ask me how I'm doing, but they couldn't care less."

"The others are laughing and joking around until I come into the room. Then they become very quiet."

Anything causing people to feel self-conscious, uneasy, or excluded will have an inhibiting effect on their contribution to an organization. Instead of focusing on performance goals, they will be thinking about how awkward and uncomfortable they feel. In my experience, an atmosphere of acceptance and inclusiveness is absolutely essential to the development of an effective team or organization.

Diagnosing and Dealing with Unmet Psychological Needs

Many negative behaviors in organizations, including resistance to change, are symptomatic of unmet psychological needs. Table 1 offers some examples of these symptoms, along with consequences of these symptoms and potential solutions. Two different kinds of symptoms can be distinguished: behaviors people shouldn't engage in but do and behaviors they should engage in but don't. The former might be called sins of commission and includes behaviors such as showing up late to meetings and making derogatory comments about others behind their backs. The latter, which we could call sins of omission, refers to behaviors such as withholding help or failing to follow through on an agreed change.

There is no one-to-one relationship between a particular symptom and an underlying cause. Instead, we should view symptoms as data that we use to formulate hypotheses about causes. Thorough data collection allows for more accuracy in the diagnosis. We can gather information about symptoms by observing people's behavior and asking them to describe what others say and do that they find troubling. When we do this, the data will start to form patterns that point toward causes. Additional information can be collected by asking such questions as these:

"Does the team/organization make full use of your knowledge and skills?"

"Do you feel your work makes a difference to the team/organization?"

"Do you feel people treat you and each other with respect?"

"Do you feel accepted by the team/organization?"

Questions targeted to specific unmet needs often strike a responsive cord, because people are seldom asked about their feelings; their comments, therefore, are often quite candid and revealing. You can also gather information about symptoms of unmet needs by administering the Psychological Need Fulfillment Inventory, which appears at the end of this chapter. A large number of and diversity of symptoms indicates the presence of two, three, or even four unmet needs. In such cases it is important to determine which need represents the most serious problem.

Consequences are the negative results stemming from symptoms. Although every problem tends to bring about lower productivity and morale, you can often trace additional consequences back to specific unmet needs. As Table 1 shows, some possible consequences of lack of respect are suspiciousness, defensiveness, and a poor team image. Gather information about consequences by observing the impact of team behavior, reviewing relevant performance data, and asking team members to describe the effects of their problems. Another useful approach is to seek input from outsiders, such as internal and external customers, suppliers, and representatives from management, who are affected by people's behavior. Often people either don't see or they minimize the importance of their issues, so becoming aware that their behavior is perceived negatively by others can serve as an incentive for them to work toward solutions.

In dealing with resistance to change one of the most common mistakes is to react to symptoms instead of actively look for solutions that deal with underlying needs. This often makes the situation worse. If people show a lack of respect by verbally attacking each other, for example, threatening them would only serve to increase defensiveness. It would be more constructive to have people generate a set of norms for how they want to be treated and then to come up with procedures for holding each other accountable when the norms are violated.

When people become polarized, it often takes the assistance of an internal or external consultant to help facilitate a process of positive change. By this time, people are usually very defensive and unable to look at their situation objectively, viewing everything from a win-lose

Table 1

Unmet Needs: Symptoms, Consequences, and Potential Solutions

Causes	Symptoms are that people . . .	Consequences	Potential Solutions
Unmet Need for *Mastery*	Expect too little from themselves	Low Productivity	Training
	Lack opportunities to use their skills	Morale problems	Coaching/counseling
	Lack the necessary knowledge or understanding	Complaints from customers	Feedback
	Struggle to keep up with changes	Missed deadlines	Ask for help
	Lack the required skill or ability	Cost overruns	Offer to help each other
	Avoid taking risks	Layoffs	Encourage others to do their best
	Make too many mistakes	Lost accounts	Empowerment
	Have trouble staying on top of the job	Bankruptcy	Look for opportunities to use everyone's skills
	Aren't encouraged to develop their skills	Frustration	Expect everyone to do their very best
	Make excuses for poor performance	Resentment	Expect everyone to be responsible for their work
	Blame each other for mistakes	Fear of failure	
	Have trouble getting enough work done		
	Have trouble with the quality of their work		
	Lack confidence in each other's ability		
	Create bottlenecks for others		

Table 1

Unmet Needs: Symptoms, Consequences, and Potential Solutions *(continued)*

Causes	Symptoms are that people. . . .	Consequences	Potential Solutions
Unmet Need for a *Sense* of *Meaning* and *Purpose*	Disagree with the goals/methods of the team	Low productivity	Job enrichment
	Disagree with each other about priorities	Morale problems	Job rotation
	Don't seem to care about their work	Turnover	Cross-training
	Feel treated like numbers, not persons	Complaints	Opportunities for advancement
	Feel their work goes unappreciated	Restlessness	Career development program
	Do the work because they have to, not because they want to	Poor reputation as a place to work	Meaningful incentives
	Lack a sense of accomplishment	Fear of purposelessness	Empowerment
	Seem to lack motivation		Involvement/Participation
	Feel their work is unimportant		Express appreciation
	Don't feel their work contributes to the team		Give recognition
	Feel their jobs are expendable		Seek people's input
	Feel unneeded by the team		Suggestion program
	Don't feel they receive enough recognition		
	Don't find their work very gratifying		
	Act like they're going through the motions		

Table 1

Unmet Needs: Symptoms, Consequences, and Potential Solutions *(continued)*

Causes	Symptoms are that people . . .	Consequences	Potential Solutions
Unmet Need for *Acceptance*	Judge each other on the basis of personal characteristics	Low productivity	Convey that discrimination is unacceptable
	Discriminate against others	Morale problems	Stress the benefits of diversity
	Subtly make others feel excluded	Work environment perceived as hostile	Emphasize people's strengths
	Don't offer to help each other	Untapped talent	Team building
	Act superior to others	Poor communication	Diversity training
	Withhold constructive feedback	Alienation, isolation	Convey that team goals can't be accomplished without everyone's help
	Withhold encouragement/support	Self-consciousness	Seek input from everyone
	Just look out for themselves	Poor team/organization image	Remove barriers to full involvement/participation
	Form themselves into camps	Lawsuits	Establish climate for open communication
	Reject those who are different	Turnover	Confront problems directly
	Have a "we-they" mentality	Fear of rejection	
	Make new employees feel unwelcome		
	Don't seem to value input from others		
	Avoid each other		
	Use favoritism to get what they want		

Table 1

Unmet Needs: Symptoms, Consequences, and Potential Solutions *(continued)*

Causes	Symptoms are that people . . .	Consequences	Potential Solutions
Unmet Need for *Respect*	Malign each other's character	Low productivity	Convey what behaviors are acceptable/unacceptable
	Withhold information from each other	Morale problems	Establish a climate for open communication
	Try to make each other look bad	Interpersonal conflict	Confront problems openly and directly
	Question each other's motives	Lack of trust	Nip problems in the bud
	Use manipulative tactics	Poor communication	Expect people to work out their differences
	Verbally attack each other	Suspiciousness	Treat others the way you want to be treated
	Say one thing but do another	Defensiveness	Stress the importance of cooperation
	Say one thing to one person, something else to another person	Posturing	Refuse to listen to gossip
	Pretend to agree with each other	Revenge/retaliation	Hold people accountable for what they say and do
	Put each other down	Polarization	
	Start rumors about each other	Poor team/organization image	
	Gossip about each other	High level of tension	
	Have hidden agendas	Turnover	
	Distort what others say	Fear of judgment	
	Aren't honest with each other		

perspective. Some will even say they're convinced that change is impossible and they've given up trying.

Summary

People are motivated to meet their various physical and psychological needs. The most important needs that people try to meet in the workplace are mastery, a sense of meaning and purpose, respect, and acceptance. These needs serve the larger purpose of helping people have a sense of worth and value, which is crucial to their personal and interpersonal effectiveness. In my experience as an OD consultant, a higher level of job satisfaction exists in organizations where people are encouraged to use their abilities and make a contribution in an atmosphere of mutual respect and acceptance than exists in organizations that neglect one or more of these key needs.

Psychological Need Fulfillment Inventory

Purpose

Unmet psychological needs are responsible for many organizational problems, including interpersonal conflict and resistance to change. The Psychological Need Fulfillment Inventory is a behaviorally based instrument designed to assess how effectively an organization meets people's psychological needs. Avoid using both the Psychological Need Fulfillment Inventory and the Team Trust Scale (see Chapter 9) with the same group of participants, because there is an overlap of items. If you're trying to choose between the two instruments, keep in mind that the former is more comprehensive, and the latter is specifically targeted to the issue of trust.

Procedure

The Psychological Need Fulfillment Inventory can be used by itself to help identify the cause(s) of resistance to change, or it can be used in conjunction with other data-collection methods, such as the Change Opinion Survey and patterned interviews. It can also be used before and after an OD intervention to evaluate its effectiveness. In addition, an individual can complete it to determine the extent to which his or her needs are being met by the organization. If considerable tension exists among the people you plan to use it with, consider having them complete it anonymously.

Mean scores for the four psychological needs can vary from 0 to 60. The higher the mean score the better. A mean score below 20 indicate a serious problem.

One way to use the data is to display the completed Psychological Need Fulfillment Profile and then facilitate a discussion of an organization/team's relative strengths and weaknesses in meeting needs. This discussion can be enhanced by calculating mean scores for individual items on the inventory and then making a list of the lowest and highest items for each need. People are usually more candid in talking about negative behaviors once the data has been presented, because it represents a consensus regarding areas of concern.

Quite often inventory results contain some very low scores. While it's important to discuss these in depth, it's also important to focus on positive behaviors, because this provides a balanced view of organizational or team functioning. This helps instill a sense of hope that problems can be solved, while lowering the chances that people will become defensive. Once problems have been identified, you can facilitate a discussion of possible solutions. Some suggestions are presented in Chapters 9 and 10.

Directions

The Psychological Need Fulfillment Inventory is designed to assess the degree to which your organization is currently meeting people's job-related psychological needs. Organizations and teams that respond to the relevant needs of people can be expected to have higher morale and, therefore, be more productive. The scores will help identify strengths and areas where improvement is needed.

Read each item on the next three pages and circle the response that best describes your opinion. The scale is a continuum from 4 to 0, with 4 meaning strongly disagree and 0 meaning strongly agree. Your responses will be combined with those of others in your team and will be kept confidential. You will receive a summary of the results once they've been compiled.

People in my organization

1. Expect too little from themselves	4	3	2	1	0
2. Malign each other's character	4	3	2	1	0
3. Judge each other on the basis of personal characteristics	4	3	2	1	0
4. Disagree about goals/methods	4	3	2	1	0
5. Lack opportunities to use their skills	4	3	2	1	0
6. Withhold information from one another	4	3	2	1	0
7. Discriminate against others	4	3	2	1	0
8. Disagree with each other about priorities	4	3	2	1	0
9. Lack the necessary knowledge or understanding	4	3	2	1	0
10. Try to make each other look bad	4	3	2	1	0
11. Subtly make others feel excluded	4	3	2	1	0
12. Don't seem to care about their work	4	3	2	1	0
13. Struggle to keep up with changes	4	3	2	1	0
14. Question each other's motives	4	3	2	1	0
15. Don't offer to help each other	4	3	2	1	0
16. Feel treated like numbers, not persons	4	3	2	1	0
17. Lack the required skill or ability	4	3	2	1	0
18. Use manipulative tactics	4	3	2	1	0
19. Act superior to others	4	3	2	1	0
20. Feel their work goes unappreciated	4	3	2	1	0
21. Avoid taking risks	4	3	2	1	0
22. Verbally attack each other	4	3	2	1	0
23. Don't give each other enough constructive feedback	4	3	2	1	0
24. Do the work because they have to, not because they want to	4	3	2	1	0
25. Make too many mistakes	4	3	2	1	0
26. Say one thing but do another	4	3	2	1	0
27. Don't give each other enough encouragement or support	4	3	2	1	0
28. Lack a sense of accomplishment in their work	4	3	2	1	0
29. Have trouble staying on top of their job	4	3	2	1	0

People in my organization

30. Say one thing to one person, something else to another person	4	3	2	1	0
31. Just look out for themselves	4	3	2	1	0
32. Seem to lack motivation	4	3	2	1	0
33. Aren't encouraged to develop their skills	4	3	2	1	0
34. Pretend to agree with each other	4	3	2	1	0
35. Form themselves into camps	4	3	2	1	0
36. Feel their work is unimportant	4	3	2	1	0
37. Make excuses for poor performance	4	3	2	1	0
38. Put each other down	4	3	2	1	0
39. Reject those who are different	4	3	2	1	0
40. Don't feel their work contributes very much	4	3	2	1	0
41. Blame each other for mistakes	4	3	2	1	0
42. Start rumors about each other	4	3	2	1	0
43. Have a "we-they" mentality	4	3	2	1	0
44. Feel their jobs are expendable	4	3	2	1	0
45. Have trouble getting enough work done	4	3	2	1	0
46. Gossip about each other	4	3	2	1	0
47. Make new employees feel unwelcome	4	3	2	1	0
48. Don't feel like they're needed	4	3	2	1	0
49. Have trouble with the quality of their work	4	3	2	1	0
50. Have hidden agendas	4	3	2	1	0
51. Don't seem to value input from others	4	3	2	1	0
52. Don't feel they receive enough recognition for their efforts	4	3	2	1	0
53. Lack confidence in each other's ability	4	3	2	1	0
54. Distort what others say	4	3	2	1	0
55. Avoid each other	4	3	2	1	0
56. Don't find their work very gratifying	4	3	2	1	0
57. Create bottlenecks for each other	4	3	2	1	0
58. Aren't honest with each other	4	3	2	1	0
59. Use favoritism to get what they want	4	3	2	1	0
60. Act like they're just going through the motions	4	3	2	1	0

Calculating Scores

This instrument consists of sixty items, fifteen pertaining to each of the psychological needs for mastery, respect, acceptance, and a sense of meaning and purpose. You can develop a Psychological Need Fulfillment Profile by following these procedures:

1. Total the scores of each team member for the four needs. Items pertaining to the needs are

   Mastery: 1, 5, 9, 13, 17, 21, 25, 29, 33, 37, 41, 45, 49, 53, 57
   Respect: 2, 6, 10, 14, 18, 22, 26, 30, 34, 38, 42, 46, 50, 54, 58
   Acceptance: 3, 7, 11, 15, 19, 23, 27, 31, 35, 39, 43, 47, 51, 55, 59
   Meaning/Purpose: 4, 8, 12, 16, 20, 24, 28, 32, 36, 40, 44, 48, 52, 56, 60

2. Add the totals of all respondents together for each need, and divide these totals by the number of respondents completing the instrument. This will give you the mean or average scores for the four needs.

3. Place a dot at the corresponding point on the profile for each need, and connect the dots with a line.

Psychological Need Fulfillment Profile

	Very Poor	Poor	Fair	Good	Very Good	Excellent
Mastery						
Respect						
Acceptance						
Meaning and Purpose						

5   10   15   20   25   30   35   40   45   50   55   60

MEAN SCORES

The Motivational Cycle

If we view needs as inputs (motives) and either fulfilled or unfulfilled needs as outputs, then we can identify four important process steps between them: thinking, feeling, deciding, and doing. Descartes said, "I think; therefore I am." My view can be summarized this way: "I need, I think, I feel, I decide, I do; therefore I am." Taken together, the input, process steps, and output form the motivational cycle, which is depicted in Figure 3. Let's look at the four process steps in depth.[1]

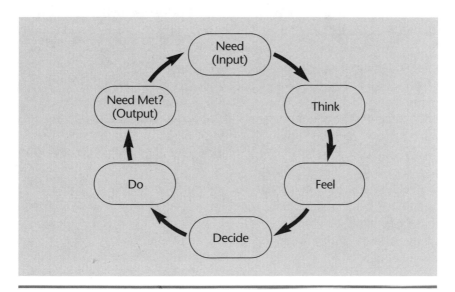

Figure 3   Motivational Cycle

Thinking

People don't act on reality, but rather on their perception of it. Perception has to do with the way we take in information from the outside world. Some people prefer to gather information through their five senses of seeing, hearing, feeling, smelling, and tasting, while others prefer to use intuition, or what is commonly called a "sixth sense." In either case, they think about the information gathered, organize it, and store it in their brain for future reference. To do this they rely on their capacity to formulate beliefs. Beliefs are subjective assumptions, conclusions, interpretations, and predictions. We can distinguish three major types of beliefs:

▲ **Descriptive beliefs** are interpretations about what is true or false ("He can't be trusted.").
▲ **Evaluative beliefs** are interpretations about what is good or bad ("Sharing that information was very unethical.").
▲ **Predictive beliefs** are interpretations about what is going to happen in the future ("He'll be acting the same way five years from now.").

As humans we are not only rational beings who seek to understand and to anticipate the future, but we are also ethical beings who seek to distinguish between right and wrong. Beliefs allow us to be both rational and ethical.

In one of the earliest psychological studies on beliefs, J. Jastrow described human beings as belief-seekers rather than fact-seekers. It's important to make a clear distinction between beliefs and facts, because people often state beliefs as though they're facts ("I know I'm right, and that's all there is to it!"). A fact is an objective reality that can be proven with complete certainty, while a belief is a subjective opinion. There are many things that you can know with certainty and legitimately refer to as facts. For example, you can know your name, age, marital status, and other vital statistics. In addition, you can know that you own a certain type of car, work for a certain organization, and earn a certain income. You can also know that certain things happened to you in the past ("I graduated from college") and that certain things are happening to you right now ("I'm driving to work"). However, once you go beyond what you can prove, which means everything in the future, you're in the realm of belief.

In the thinking process, beliefs are usually more important than facts because they represent the interpretations drawn from factual information. We all know that facts are subject to distortion; two people exposed to the same set of facts can arrive at entirely different conclusions about what they mean. Nevertheless, most of us hold beliefs with such confidence that we treat them as facts. Such beliefs are difficult to change because we regard them as absolute and indisputable conclusions. We are assuming that our beliefs and reality are identical. In one sense, this is true. Our beliefs are our way of understanding ourselves, other people, and the world around us. In essence, our beliefs become our reality. It is a mistake, however, to conclude that our beliefs represent the one and only concept of reality.

A related dynamic is that often we *want* to believe that our beliefs are accurate.[2] In other words, we have a vested interest in our beliefs. For many of us, questioning our beliefs is tantamount to challenging our ability to accurately understand reality. This is usually an anxiety-provoking experience, one that people try to avoid. When beliefs are challenged or contradicted by new evidence, people often become defensive and refuse to acknowledge, either to themselves or to others, that their beliefs may be inaccurate. Such expressions as "Don't confuse me with the facts" show the stubbornness with which people hold on to beliefs in spite of contrary evidence.

This is not to imply that people have the same degree of confidence in all their beliefs. Beliefs that are consistently successful in interpreting present experiences or predicting the future are held with more confidence and are more resistant to change than beliefs that are not so successful. Less reliable beliefs are more readily subjected to scrutiny and change as people attempt to become more successful at meeting their needs. The belief you have about your ability to drive to work safely will probably be held with considerable confidence and will resist change, unless you have an accident. Then you may decide to reassess your beliefs about driving, and taking the bus may not seem as inconvenient as it did before.

While it's true that people formulate beliefs to account for all their experiences, some beliefs have more impact than others. For our purposes, the most important beliefs are those people hold about themselves, other people, and the organization. Let's examine these three major categories of beliefs.

Beliefs About Self

Everyone must formulate beliefs that answer fundamental questions such as "Who am I?" "What are my capabilities?" "How am I different from others?" and "What are my unique qualities?" Seeking answers to these and other questions about the self is a lifelong process. A child's beliefs about self are much more tentative than those of an adult, but even an adult's beliefs are not immune to change; adults continue to have new experiences, regardless of age. Since beliefs about the self are fluid, we should be encouraged about the possibility of overcoming resistance to change in others.

To a great extent, the fulfillment people experience in life depends upon whether their sense of self-worth is high or low. It would be incongruent to find people with low self-worth spending a lot of time and energy developing their potential. They simply don't see any potential to develop. People's experiences and interpretations of those experiences are crucial in determining their views regarding their worth or lack of worth. People cannot simply coax themselves into positive beliefs about self that are independent of their experiences. Those who attempt to do this are regarded as being out of touch with reality. Instead, a set of positive views about one's worth must be won in the real world, with successful experiences. Fulfillment must be related to actual achievements in order to be real. Providing people with an opportunity to have what they regard as success in an area that has been characterized by failure may help them change beliefs about what they can do. This, in turn, may enable them to achieve something that previously would have been considered impossible.

In the work environment, people's beliefs about their competence are usually the most significant factor in determining their sense of self-worth. As with other beliefs, competence must be demonstrated in the real world. It would be difficult for people to develop an accurate set of beliefs about their competence without external validation from others. For example, it would be hard to see how I could consider myself an effective consultant if no one hired me. At some point, the concept I have about my competence must correlate with the views of other people. We have little patience with people who profess to be competent, but prove in actual practice to be incompetent. We expect people to hold views of themselves that stand up under scrutiny.

While it is important for a correlation to exist between our views of our competence and the way others view us, it is also important that we not be totally dependent upon the views of others. Children and some adults hold concepts of their competence that are almost completely dependent upon feedback from others. It is difficult for these people to think about themselves independent of others' opinions. Before acting, they try to determine whether or not their actions will meet with others' approval. Choices that might not be accepted by others are abandoned in favor of safer alternatives. In essence, these people are saying, "I am what others want me to be." We call such people codependent.

At the other extreme are people who maintain beliefs about their competence that are entirely independent of the views of others. These people fall into one of two categories: those who profess to be competent even though others don't share this opinion, and those who claim to be incompetent in spite of evidence to the contrary. Both groups of people are very frustrating to work with. In essence, they are saying, "I am what I am regardless of what others think."

The truth is somewhere between these extremes. A belief in one's competence usually requires external validation to be sound. At the same time, however, the belief must be independent enough of the views of others to allow for creativity and risk-taking. Over time, people usually gain enough external validation to define clear areas of competence. This can help them remain confident in spite of occasional failure experiences or criticism from others. It is my predictive belief that people who have a strong sense of self-worth, grounded in an accurate assessment of their competence, will participate more positively in change than people who don't.

Beliefs About Others

Next to beliefs about ourselves, nothing is so central to fulfillment and productivity than the nature of our beliefs about others. As I mentioned earlier, it's virtually impossible to get our needs met apart from other people. Our day-to-day behavior consists of meeting the needs of others and having others meeting our needs. On the job it means working together to get things done, especially during these times when teams are being emphasized so strongly. When teams are functioning smoothly, there is harmonious interdependence among people. A lack of such interdependence usually leads to conflict. Beliefs about others are key ingredients in determining whether harmony or conflict is the outcome of interpersonal relationships.

People can form beliefs about individuals ("You can't trust him"), specific groups of people ("You can't trust whites"), and all humanity ("You can't trust people"). Beliefs about others can be an asset or a liability. If continually assessed for accuracy and modified to account for new information, beliefs help people know what to expect from each other. For example, a manager may believe that although there are exceptions, most employees want to do a good job. This belief may improve the ability of the manager to relate constructively to individual employees. It may also improve employee response.

Conversely, people's beliefs can have a negative impact on relationships. When people meet, they form impressions of each other, primarily to determine if others can be trusted. There is nothing wrong with this process per se. In fact, needs for safety, acceptance, and respect probably dictate that people resolve the question of trust before moving ahead with other matters. There is a problem, however, when conclusions about the trustworthiness of others are based on inaccurate, incomplete, or distorted information. This creates an environment in which people are on guard against each other. Since people's suspicions are seldom discussed openly, relationships can become permanently tainted by mistrust. Testing the accuracy of facts and beliefs can prevent this from happening. A stereotype is an example of a conclusion that has a negative impact on relationships. Stereotypes greatly diminish the likelihood that people will be able to relate to others as unique individuals.

Sometimes people form conclusions about others under one set of circumstances and assume mistakenly that they will be valid under different circumstances. At other times people retain conclusions valid in the past, even though changes render the conclusions invalid in the present. Look at the statement "People will never appreciate what I do for this organization." Most likely, it is based on the past. Although it may be backed up by substantial evidence, assuming that it will be true in the future may prevent one from noticing new behavior that could modify this belief. Often it is difficult to do anything about such beliefs because people seldom reveal them.

I once had a colleague who had a sticker on his door that said ASSUME NOTHING! This is good advice. It is important to notice changes in other people so that we can bring our beliefs about them into line with present reality. In addition, we must be aware of their potential for change before we can help them develop their full potential.

Beliefs About the Organization

In addition to beliefs about self and others, beliefs about the organization are important in determining people's behavior. These can be divided into two categories: beliefs about working conditions and beliefs about the interpersonal environment. Working conditions have to do with the availability and allocation of material and human resources, such as staff, money, time, equipment, supplies, training, and opportunities for advancement. Also included here are beliefs about the terms of one's employment, such as pay, benefits, performance expectations, and authority to match responsibility.

Interpersonal environment includes beliefs about management, supervisory methods, the usefulness of performance feedback, the flow of information, the degree of formality, and the amount of fairness, cooperation, encouragement, and support. These beliefs, which are significant in defining the corporate culture, address the question, "How do things get done around here?" As a result of its culture, an organization can take on a personality, and employees are expected to conform to this personality. For example, I've been in organizations that have a "macho" personality, where most employees talk and act rough and sexual harassment is encouraged or at least tolerated. Corporate culture is difficult to change because, "That's just the way we do things around here." In other words, the subject isn't open to discussion. When someone challenges the culture of an organization, employees rally together to defend it.

Examples of statements reflecting beliefs about the interpersonal environment of an organization are as follows:

"In order to succeed in this organization, you have to . . ."

"If you make a mistake, you can never live it down."

"Management doesn't care what we think."

"We like to have a relaxed, informal atmosphere."

"They never tell us anything."

"They talk about quality for the customer, but all they care about is money."

"You can never tell what management will do next."

"Be very careful what you tell the marketing department."

"The only time we hear from upper management is when there's trouble."

Beliefs are central to everything done in organizations. Performance goals and standards are based on beliefs about the amount of work people can do. Salary scales are based on beliefs about the worth of different types of work. Marketing campaigns are based largely on beliefs about what the competition is going to do. In a cost/benefit analysis, costs have to do with facts and beliefs, while benefits have to do with values, which I discuss later in this chapter. Long-range plans and business forecasts are based on beliefs about future organizational performance; contingency plans represent beliefs about what to do if the predictions turn out to be wrong. Problem solving and decision making hinge on the accuracy of beliefs. Without beliefs organizations could not exist, let alone fulfill their purposes.

Feeling

Thinking is a cognitive process, guided chiefly by facts and beliefs. There is a strong relationship between the cognitive process of thinking, on the one hand, and feelings, on the other. Feelings have to do with emotions. Without feelings we might be able to think, but we would respond like robots. By themselves facts are neutral—they don't elicit any feelings. One person could look at a set of facts and say, "So what," while another person might say, "Oh no!" It is the assumptions, conclusions, interpretations, and predictions we draw from facts that give rise to feelings.[3] We know that the perception of danger, both real and imagined, can evoke anxiety and fear. In the same way, negative beliefs about self, others, or the organization can produce negative emotions such as depression, discouragement, helplessness, hopelessness, despair, pessimism, hurt, frustration, anger, resentment, hate, guilt, and shame. In contrast, positive thoughts can produce a wide range of positive emotions, such as enthusiasm, excitement, hope, optimism, confidence, love, joy, happiness, satisfaction, and fulfillment. Some examples of beliefs and likely feelings are shown in Table 2.

Most people would agree that there is a relationship between thoughts and feelings. There is much debate, however, on whether feelings are causes or effects. My view is that while feelings can occur at any point during the motivational cycle, they are most important as the consequences (effects) of thinking and as motivators (causes) for decisions. Empirically based, rational beliefs lead to positive feelings, while non-empirically based, irrational beliefs evoke negative feelings. Feelings can have a powerful impact on our decisions. Feelings such as depression, hopelessness,

Table 2

Examples of Beliefs and Associated Feelings

Beliefs	Likely Feelings
"I'll never be able to do this."	Helplessness, hopelessness, discouragement, frustration
"Be careful what you say; he might use it against you."	Fear, anger, bitterness, suspicion
"Our products are inferior to theirs."	Pessimism, discouragement, frustration, uselessness, futility
"Management seems to be encouraging creativity and innovativeness."	Encouragement, enthusiasm
"This change will only make things worse."	Anger, frustration
"I think they're trying to find a way to get rid of people."	Fear, anger, resentment, hate
"They don't care what I think."	Hurt, discouragement, depression
"I'm trapped in this organization."	Helplessness, hopelessness, despair
"Teams will never work here."	Skepticism, pessimism, frustration
"It looks like they need what I have to offer."	Enthusiasm, excitement
"Together, we'll find a solution to this problem."	Confidence, optimism
"Nobody's interested in working with me."	Loneliness, isolation, depression, discouragement

helplessness, shame, and guilt tend to be demotivating, while fear, anger, confidence, and enthusiasm can be very motivating. The way people deal with feelings plays a key role in determining the extent to which their decisions will be based on rational or emotional considerations.

Deciding

So far, we've talked about needs and about how thinking and feeling affect our efforts to meet needs. As if this weren't complicated enough, there is another factor we must consider in order to understand human motivation—deciding. Deciding has to do with *values,* which are beliefs about what is important in life.[4] Values represent the criteria or standards we use in making decisions. Thus, decisions reveal values. When considering a number of alternatives, we eliminate the ones that don't meet our criteria. Values also allow us to set priorities, reflecting what we regard as being most important.

Values are to people what instincts are to animals. Since animals can think and feel in varying degrees, it is the ability to decide based on values that sets human beings apart. Without the capacity to choose values, we could not be held accountable for our actions.

Perhaps an example will highlight the role of values in deciding. Let's say that my miniature schnauzer, Princess, and I are stranded on a desert island and I have only a two-day supply of water. I weigh two alternatives. First, I can keep all the water for myself, giving me forty-eight hours to wait for help. This means that Princess will die unless we are rescued today. Second, I can share the water with her, giving us both twenty-four hours to be rescued.

As I lean toward the first alternative, Princess looks up at me with her trusting eyes and I am filled with both compassion and guilt. Since she has been a loyal companion for many years, which I value highly, I decide to share the water with her. I deny my need for a higher purpose. To celebrate my decision, a triumph of the human spirit, I run along the beach for several minutes shouting for joy. On my return, I am shocked and bewildered to discover that Princess has lapped up all the water, oblivious to the fact that she has sealed my doom. I think to myself, "You dumb animal!" but then I remember that she is only acting on her instinct to survive.

Consider the relationship between thinking and deciding. While thinking has to do with the mind, deciding has to do with the will. The mind and the will are two separate but interrelated aspects of psychological functioning. Although people usually rely on facts and beliefs to make decisions, this isn't always the case. For example, let's say that two people know many facts about the effects of smoking, believe that smoking is harmful (descriptive belief), believe that smoking is morally wrong (evaluative belief), and believe that smoking eventually will cause health problems (predictive belief), but one of them decides to smoke anyway. To understand the difference between the two, we would have to know something about their values. More than likely, the person deciding to smoke places a lower value on health than the other one.

An evaluative belief is similar to a value, but there is a key difference. Evaluative beliefs represent what we refer to as shoulds, oughts, and musts. In contrast, values refer to what we consider to be important. In many instances, people's evaluative beliefs and their values are consistent ("I've decided to move forward with affirmative action because it's the right thing to do"). In other instances, however, people's evaluative beliefs and their values are inconsistent ("I know I shouldn't say this, but I think it's important to be honest"). People can think something's good but still not do it, and they can think something's bad but do it anyway.

Discrepancies between what people say they believe and their behavior are quite common and accepted as a normal part of life. This makes the practice of predicting people's behavior highly precarious. Facts and beliefs *may* affect our actions, but by definition, values *must* be connected to what we do. Psychologist Milton Rokeach says that values are imperatives for action. They represent preferred ways of meeting needs. It simply doesn't make sense to say, "This is what I prefer," and then not act on it. A distinction can be made, therefore, between genuine values and bogus values. A *genuine value* is one that actually guides a person's behavior, while a *bogus value* is one that the person claims to hold but doesn't act on. Thus, someone acting on genuine values is said to be "walking the talk." In contrast, someone stating bogus values is said to be manipulative and untrustworthy or indecisive.

Some examples of bogus values are as follows:

▲ Some organizations say they value quality, but they actually value efficiency, and striving for quality is used as an excuse to downsize and cut costs.
▲ Some organizations say they value teamwork, but they actually reward individual performance at the expense of team performance.
▲ Some organizations say they value affirmative action, but the number of women and minorities they have in key positions represents tokenism.
▲ Some organizations say they value empowerment, but only suggestions from supervisors and managers are given serious consideration.

Bogus values often are easy to spot—discrepancies between what people say and do shine like beacons—but they're hard to change, because they become deeply rooted in the corporate culture. Bringing bogus values out in the open and discussing them is very important, however, because as long as they remain hidden they contribute to cynicism, mistrust, and low morale within the workforce.

Even if we know people's facts, beliefs, and values, we still can't say for sure what they will do. One of the reasons for this is that there is no accounting for the will. We're all familiar with the expression "Where there's a will there's a way." Just when you think you have people figured out, they do the unexpected. People are capable of rising to the occasion and performing acts of heroism that surprise even themselves. They will risk anything, even death, to pursue something they care about passionately. When consulting assignments take me to organizations undergoing large-scale change, invariably I encounter people who say such things as, "I wouldn't have been able to get through this if it hadn't been for my religious faith," "I was about to give up when I found an inner strength I didn't know was there," or "I got tired of people walking all over me." I've been inspired by people who have shown courage under tremendous pressure. They have taught me to respect people's will, and to avoid underestimating what people can accomplish. Problems that look overwhelming can be instrumental in building self-confidence, as people meet them head-on and affirm what they believe is important.

Earlier I mentioned that facts are neutral and that it is the beliefs drawn from facts that give rise to feelings. I stated that feelings are primarily consequences of beliefs and that feelings can have a powerful impact on decisions. We all know people who, while normally logical and rational, are capable of making impulsive or irrational decisions when upset. There's a lot of wisdom to the saying that logic and emotions don't mix. Feelings not only influence values, but values can also evoke feelings. This is because nothing has intrinsic value to people. Rather, people ascribe value based on what they decide is important. People care about their values; they feel good about experiences that affirm their values and bad about experiences that negate their values. As with beliefs, people develop a vested interest in their values; they want to believe that their values are the true ones, the best ones, the only ones.

A value is also influenced by its opposite. Milton Rokeach defined a value as a preference for one thing over its opposite. He reasoned that if people prefer one thing, they will be against its opposite. Thus, a value and its opposite are dichotomous or mutually exclusive. Psychologically, it's not possible to want something and its opposite at the same time without having a multiple personality. Some examples of such dichotomies are security versus risk taking, independence versus dependence, and recognition versus anonymity.

Although values can be described as dichotomous, in reality it is extremely difficult to be totally supportive of a value. For example, no one takes risks all the time. At any moment, a person is somewhere on a continuum between risk taking and security. One day they be may lean toward risk taking and the next day toward security. The same principle applies to all our values. I address this issue again in Part 2, when I discuss the intensity of resistance.

While values can inspire people to overcome obstacles, they can also have a negative impact on thinking. The issue can be stated this way: if people want something badly enough, they're capable of aligning the mind to fit the will. People are willing to take more risks to accomplish something important to them, and sometimes they take too great a risk. We all know people who ignore or minimize facts in an attempt to justify their actions to themselves and others. In the face of contrary evidence, they say such things as, "Oh, that's no problem," "I can deal with that," "It doesn't matter how much it costs," or "We can train him." In the psychological literature, this process is referred to as *rationalization*. When people engage in this practice, onlookers often say they are out of touch with reality. People make decisions they later regret when they rationalize facts or assert beliefs based on inaccurate or distorted information.

According to Dr. Morris Massey, about 90 percent of our values are programmed by our surroundings by the time we are about ten years old. He maintains that each generation develops and programs a set of values that people then try to impose on others. Thus, we had Baby Boomers, Hippies, and Yuppies, and, more recently, Generation X. When individuals with one value system attempt to influence individuals with another, often there is conflict. Even within one generation, no two people have exactly the same value system. Much of the richness and diversity among people comes from differences in values and the various ways that values are expressed. For our purposes, the most important values are those pertaining to the self, other people, and the organization. Let's examine these categories separately.

Values Pertaining to the Self (Personal Values)

Examples of values focusing on the self are ambition, achievement, courage, creativity, health, recreation, happiness, self-understanding, knowledge, and power. A person may embrace a combination of these and other values, but time limits how much they can be pursued.

Therefore, people must decide to place a higher priority on some values than others. The direction people take in life and what they accomplish depends largely upon the priority assigned to various personal values.

Perhaps an example will show how pursuing one value affects attention that could be devoted to other values. To prepare for careers in professional fields such as medicine and law, people are required to successfully complete a rigorous educational program. They would need to place high priority on achievement and postpone or forego other values, such as friendship, to obtain the necessary education. Some people may not be willing to make the sacrifices required to earn a degree in one of these fields, because they give priority to other values.

The personal values of employees will have a great effect on their behavior at work. For example, some employees place a high value on a strong work ethic, while others are satisfied to just get by because their values are elsewhere ("I live for the weekend"). Although there are exceptions, employees are usually more productive and reliable if they take pride in their work. Initiatives designed to increase the degree of employee ownership is one of the most effective ways to help an organization achieve its goals.

Values Pertaining to Others (Social Values)

Since people are interdependent in meeting their needs, they must not only consider what they want but what others want. Self-centered people don't get very far and certainly aren't held in high esteem or trusted by others. The interpersonal climate of an organization can have a profound impact on productivity and morale. With the current emphasis on teamwork and networking in organizations, relationship building can make the difference between career success and failure. Accordingly, people who value cooperation, mutual interest, fairness, participation, and equality are likely to be more successful than those who don't.

One of my major areas of specialization as a consultant is working with teams experiencing intense interpersonal conflict. When I first arrive, usually I find team members polarized into camps, and the climate is characterized by mistrust, hostility, and poor communication. While I use a variety of interventions in an effort to improve interpersonal relationships, the thrust of my work is to help team members place greater emphasis on appropriate social values.

Values Pertaining to the Organization

There are many things in organizations that are driven by values. A mission statement showcases the values of an organization. It says, "This is who we are; this is what we're about." A vision also expresses values; it describes what the organization wants to become. It says, "This is what we think is important in the future." Jack Welch, General Electric's CEO, outlined this vision (emphasis is mine):

> The winners of the Nineties will be those who can develop a culture that allows them to *move faster, communicate more clearly, and involve everyone* in a focused effort to serve ever more demanding customers. To move toward that winning culture we've got to create what we call a *"boundaryless" company.* We no longer have the time to climb over barriers between functions like engineering and marketing, or between people—hourly, salaried, management, and the like. *Geographic barriers must evaporate.* Our people must be as comfortable in Delhi and Seoul as they are in Louisville and Schenectady. The lines between the company and its vendors and customers must be blurred into a smooth, fluid process with no other objective than *satisfying the customer* and *winning in the marketplace.* If we are to get the reflexes and speed we need, we've got to *simplify* and *delegate* more—simply *trust* more. We need to drive *self-confidence* deep into the organization. A company can't distribute self-confidence, but it can foster it by removing layers and giving people a chance to win. We have to undo a 100-year-old concept and convince our managers that their role is not to control people and stay "on top" of things, but rather to *guide, energize, and excite.* . . . The Eighties had no shortage of individual business heroes. In the Nineties the heroes, the winners, will be entire companies that have developed cultures that instead of fearing the pace of change *relish* it.[5]

An organization's genuine values are revealed by what it rewards and punishes. Mission and vision statements are meaningless unless employees are held accountable for putting the values behind them into action. Otherwise, they're just words on a sheet of paper—bogus values. General Electric has invested a great deal of time and effort into training programs designed to help employees implement Welch's vision.

Earlier, I said that in a cost/benefit analysis, costs are facts and beliefs, while benefits are values. During decision making, people try to find the option that gives them the most of what they want (value) for the least cost. The same principle applies to buying decisions. During sales training programs, participants are taught to emphasize the benefits of their products or services. Salespeople will labor in vain unless they can relate a product or service to what prospective customers believe is important. In fact, no matter what we're trying to accomplish, whether it's selling a product or service, selling ideas, or even selling change, we'll be more successful if we take people's values into consideration.

Doing

Doing, or behaving, determines output in the motivational cycle. Doing is different from deciding. People refer to deciding as making up one's mind, but as we've seen, it's actually making up one's will. Doing is the actual implementation of decisions; it's where "the rubber meets the road." As with feelings, people disagree about whether doing is a cause or an effect. While it's true that feedback from doing can and does cause changes in people's thinking, feeling, and deciding, our focus will be on doing as the outcome of deciding.

In evaluating behavior, I've found that the most useful approach is to ask whether or not it was effective in meeting needs. People can talk all they want about their facts, beliefs, feelings, and values, but in the final analysis, it's behavior that determines whether or not needs are met. If our behavior fails to meet our needs, we're left to regroup and try again. This is the reality with which we all must contend.

Summary

The purpose of human behavior is to meet needs. In the workplace, the most important needs are for mastery, respect, belonging, and a sense of meaning and purpose. In the motivational cycle, needs are inputs, and fulfilled or unfulfilled needs are the outputs. Between the inputs and outputs are the key process steps of thinking, feeling, deciding, and doing. In the thinking process, the most important factors are facts, beliefs about what's true or false (descriptive beliefs), beliefs about what's good or bad (evaluative beliefs), and beliefs about what's going to happen in the future (predictive beliefs). In the deciding process, the most important factors are a person's values. While thinking, feeling, deciding, and behaving all mediate each other, the most practical approach is to view thinking and deciding as causes and to view feelings and behavior as effects. Thus, if we want to understand why people do what they do, and why they either change or resist change, our best bet is to examine their facts, beliefs, and values.

The Dynamics of Change

As human beings we strive to meet our needs within a context of perpetual change. Nothing remains the same from one moment to the next. We are older than we were a minute ago, and that minute is gone forever. Although dramatic events make us more aware of change at some times than others, change is constant. We can be sure of not only death and taxes but also change.

The kinds of change on which this book focuses are changes that we initiate or that we want others to make. For our purposes, change can be defined as *thinking or doing something new or differently.* Experiencing the new and different is essential to the learning process. For a newborn child *everything* is new. Almost immediately, parents begin teaching children beliefs and values, a process that is expedited by the development of language. Naturally curious, children begin exploring their world, "reality testing" their parents' beliefs and values. They learn from pain (punishment), such as when they put their hands on a hot stove they were warned not to touch, as well as from pleasure (positive reinforcement), such as when they're praised for earning good grades. Beliefs and values that meet their needs are reinforced and then resist change; beliefs and values that fail to meet their needs are discarded in favor of more satisfying alternatives.

By the time children reach the age of eighteen, they have developed thousands of beliefs about what is true and what is false, what is good and what is bad, and what is going to happen in the future. They have also formulated a set of values about what is important in life. These beliefs and values are not cast in concrete, however. What children learned within the sheltered context of their parents' home is put to the test when they leave to build a life of their own. Being exposed to the outside world challenges some of their earlier thinking. During this transition from adolescence to adulthood, referred to as *individuation,* some children change very little while others change drastically.

Children need a certain amount of security to foster their emotional and social adjustment. Moving too fast or too far into the unfamiliar will bring about a feeling of insecurity and will create resistance. Security is especially important in determining whether or not other people can be trusted. Nevertheless, security is not an end in itself, but rather a means for building a foundation from which children can venture out to meet other important social and psychological needs. The same is true for adults. Each stage of life contains special development challenges. These challenges must be faced for people to grow, and change is a necessary part of this growth process.

As I mentioned in Chapter 2, people's core psychological need is to have a sense of worth and value as a person. It is difficult for people to develop a sense of self-worth unless they view themselves as possessing courage. People feel courageous when they confront their fears and take risks and thus enhance their self-confidence and sense of worth. In contrast, people feel cowardly when fear keeps them from taking risks, which lowers their self-confidence and sense of worth. Viewing oneself as a coward leads to feelings of shame and humiliation ("Why was I afraid to do that?" "Why am I so weak?"), and people will often take risks simply to avoid such negative feelings. Thus, there's a lot of truth to the saying "No guts, no glory."

Closing the gap between one's current and one's potential performance is impossible without some risk taking. Indeed, one of the most important aspects of parenting is encouraging children to take appropriate risks. After conquering a fear, a child beams proudly, "I did it!" It happens the same way for adults as it does for children. I've seen older workers, convinced that "you can't teach an old dog a new trick," develop renewed self-confidence after learning a new skill, such as using a computer.

Sometimes people change because they want to be challenged, involved, and stimulated. Boredom can be just as motivating as the desire to accomplish a goal and can lure people into new areas. It is commonplace, for example, for people to change jobs because they're seeking a new challenge. Someone once said, "When you can't grow, you've got to go." I often change the way I conduct a workshop just to make the experience more interesting for me. While experimentation broadens my training skills, the underlying motive is to enjoy myself more fully. I suspect that a lot of the innovations we marvel at stem from people's desire to "try something different."

It's important to remember that change has both an external and an internal component. Change *must* manifest itself externally as some kind of behavior to qualify as change. In other words, people haven't changed unless they act differently. Nevertheless, external or behavioral change is *always* preceded by internal change, that is, changes in facts, beliefs, or values. For the internal change to be meaningful, it must result in behavior changes. Let's look first at the important role of facts, beliefs, and values in the change process and then at the role of behavior.

The Role of Facts and Beliefs

In Chapter 3, I indicated that facts are objective realities that can be proven with complete certainty, while beliefs are subjective variables that go beyond what can be proven. I also indicated that beliefs are more important than facts, because they are the assumptions, conclusions, interpretations, and predictions derived from factual information. To put it succinctly, beliefs represent the *meaning* people give to facts. We get used to the facts or objective realities in our lives, and the meanings we attach to them. We operate as though our facts and beliefs are accurate unless we're confronted with evidence to the contrary.

For example, let's say that every year you go for a physical exam and your blood pressure has always been in the normal range. As a result, you haven't restricted your diet, feeling free to indulge your craving for ice cream and pizza. This year, however, your physician informs you, "Your blood pressure has gone up. I think you could bring it down by changing your diet. Besides, it looks like you would afford to shed a few pounds." Stunned by this turn of events, you ask, "What will happen if I don't change my diet?" After pondering the question for several seconds, the physician replies, "That's hard to say for sure, but there's a good chance that you could develop a serious health problem." The only fact here is that your blood pressure is elevated. The other statements made by the physician are beliefs.

Recall that there are three types of beliefs: descriptive beliefs, which are interpretations about what is true and what is false; evaluative beliefs, which are interpretations about what is good and what is bad; and predictive beliefs, which are interpretations about what is going to happen in the future. We can classify the statements made by the physician as follows:

▲ "Your blood pressure has gone up" (fact).
▲ "I think you could bring it down by changing your diet" (descriptive beiief).
▲ "Besides, it looks like you could afford to shed a few pounds" (evaluative belief).
▲ "That's hard to say for sure, but there's a good chance that you could develop a serious health problem" (predictive belief).

New facts or changes in facts can have a tremendous impact on beliefs. If you have taken it for granted that you would always have low blood pressure, discovering that you now have high blood pressure will force you to reassess your beliefs and your diet.

Perhaps a work-related example will help further clarify the role of facts and beliefs in change. Let's say that you're the national sales manager for a large manufacturing company. Sales have gone up steadily over the past five years, and you don't see anything to indicate that this trend won't continue. Therefore, you draft a memo to the field sales staff that you plan to send the next morning. Here is the text of the memo:

> Our sales have grown steadily for five consecutive years. Our success has been due largely to your efforts. We should be proud to sell our products, because they're superior to anything else on the market. There's no reason to think that our sales won't continue increasing indefinitely. Therefore, I'm going to ask Bob to approve the addition of ten new sales positions to our field operations. As soon as he gives me a decision, I'll let you know. Keep up the good work!

We can decipher the memo as follows:

▲ "Our sales have gone up steadily for five consecutive years" (fact).
▲ "Our success has been due largely to your efforts" (descriptive belief).
▲ "We should be proud to sell our products, because they're superior to anything else on the market" (evaluative belief).
▲ "There's no reason to think that our sales won't continue increasing indefinitely" (predictive belief).

The next morning Bob calls you into his office and hands you the fourth-quarter sales report, which reveals plunging sales in several key markets. This new fact challenges the beliefs expressed in your memo. You will have to rewrite the memo and ponder the wisdom of asking for ten additional positions. You may also start to wonder if there's a connection between this type of situation and your increasing blood pressure.

A person's facts, descriptive beliefs, and evaluative beliefs almost always play a role in change, but in my experience, the key role is played by predictive beliefs. When people are contemplating change, the bottom line can be expressed by this question: "What impact will the change have on me?" Some people want a guarantee that a change will lead to positive results, but no such guarantee is possible. The most troubling thing to people about change is the uncertainty associated with it. Since people can't *know* what's going to happen in the future, they're forced to rely on predictive beliefs.

My concept of predictive belief is similar to others discussed in the psychological literature. For example, Kurt Lewin placed a great deal of emphasis on the relationship between the subjective probability that people give to achieving a certain goal and their behavior. E. C. Tolman concluded that people develop "cognitive maps" that serve as expectancies regarding the anticipated consequences of behavior. Similarly, E. Brunswik held that a person formulates "probabilistic expectancies" that function as guidelines for action. Alfred Adler developed his individual psychology around the premise that people are motivated primarily by their subjective expectations or beliefs regarding the future. Many other writers have discussed the relationship between predictive beliefs and subsequent behavior.

Recall that people are simultaneously motivated to meet their needs and to prevent bad things from happening to them. As a result, anticipating or predicting the probable outcomes of their actions is extremely important to their success in life. Since people can never be absolutely sure how their actions will turn out, risk is associated with everything they do. There is no escaping this reality. There is risk in acting, but there is also risk in not acting ("What will happen if I do this?" "What will happen if I don't do this?"). Inaction doesn't make people immune from risk. Similarly, there is risk in change, but there is also risk in not changing ("What will happen if I change?" "What will happen if I don't change?"). Staying the same doesn't make people immune from risk. Nevertheless, people vary greatly in the degree of

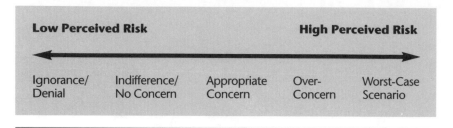

Figure 4   Predictive Belief Continuum

risk or anticipated cost they perceive in any given situation. Some people see gloom and doom around every corner, while others see a silver lining. In a team meeting where members are discussing a possible change, some may see a great deal of risk, while others may see little or no risk. The discussion can turn to conflict as members try to get their point of view across.

As shown in Figure 4, the Predictive Belief Continuum, the degree of risk people perceive in any given situation can range from none at all to extremely high. When we contemplate change, an appropriate degree of concern is necessary to avoid mistakes, but people are capable of either underestimating or overestimating risks. Those who underestimate risks usually regret their action ("Why did I do that?"), while those who overestimate risks usually regret their inaction ("Why didn't I do that?"). Since the outcome of change is always uncertain, it's natural for people to consider the worst-case scenario, if only briefly. It can become a serious problem, however, if people treat the worst-case scenario as an imminent reality when the probability of its occurrence is actually quite remote. Aaron Beck refers to this as "catastrophizing."

To avoid either underestimating or overestimating risks, it's essential to have access to accurate facts and rational, empirically based, descriptive, evaluative, and predictive beliefs. Effective risk management, contingency plans, and feasibility studies would be impossible without such data. Inaccurate facts and irrational, non-empirically based beliefs undermine efforts to plan change. People who underestimate risks won't have enough fear *(fools rush in where angels fear to tread)*, while those who overestimate risks will have too much fear *(when you borrow trouble, the interest is always paid in fear)*. Either way, the organization's ability to get where it wants to go is diminished.

The Role of Values

We could know all about people's facts, descriptive beliefs, evaluative beliefs, and predictive beliefs, but to understand why they either resist change or don't resist change, we also need to know about their values. Recall that values are beliefs, but they're different from other types of beliefs. Whereas descriptive, evaluative, and predictive beliefs have to do with the mind, values have to do with the will. Values represent what we consider to be important in life. Therefore, values perform a gatekeeping function. We screen facts and beliefs through our values before deciding what to do. People are capable of logically and rationally considering relevant facts and beliefs before acting on their values, but they're also capable of minimizing or distorting facts and beliefs to rationalize decisions to pursue their values.

Some people are more open to change, because they hold values for such things as personal growth, creativity, innovativeness, novelty, and being on the cutting edge. These people are vulnerable to underestimating the risks of change. Their reaction to proposed change is often accompanied by the words, "Why not?" Here are some of the ways they express their values:

"I'm not going to let those figures hold me back; this is what I want to do."

"If we just see the problems, we'll miss out on the opportunities."

"We can't be controlled by current conditions; we need to look to the future."

"I'm not as concerned about those projections as you are."

Divide and Conquer

Sandra Thomas started a commercial art company ten years ago. Business had been good, permitting her to expand to twenty-five employees at three locations. However, business began declining because the city wasn't growing as rapidly as it had, and competition was keener.

To avoid cutting staff, Sandra needed a way to revitalize her company. She decided to develop a retail graphic product with good sales potential. After surveying the local market, she found a demand for greeting cards incorporating local humor. In discussing this with her accountant, both concluded that producing greeting cards could lift company revenue.

There were three key people on Sandra's management team: Jerry Stephenson (Sales), Martha Gould (Art), and Carl Holt (Production). At a regular meeting, Sandra presented the greeting card idea. Although Sandra was excited about it, she encountered strong and unexpected resistance from all three managers. Jerry said producing greeting cards would detract from current efforts to increase sales (predictive belief). Martha admitted that she wasn't interested in greeting cards and suggested that the company explore other ways to boost sales (value). Finally, Carl said that the project was too complex to be successful (descriptive belief).

Even though Sandra had provided limited information, all three seemed convinced that the project was unworthy or risky. Since she needed everyone's support for the project, she realized that she had to address each person's concerns. Because Martha's objection was general and vague, Sandra began with her. She suggested to Martha that designing greeting cards might stimulate new creativity and imagination among her staff. After this discussion, Martha began to support her against the others' criticism.

Although concerned with different issues, Jerry and Carl's negative comments seemed to reflect fear that producing greeting cards could jeopardize the company—a worst-case scenario. To reduce these fears, Sandra involved the team in a variation of contingency planning called down-side planning. The team had used this method in the past to good effect. It involved generating a list of things that might go wrong and developing strategies to deal with each possible negative outcome. During this process, Jerry saw that selling greeting cards would not interfere with selling their other products. Carl discovered that although the project was complex, it could be broken down into distinct tasks that were similar to ones they were doing already.

When this process was complete, everyone expressed more confidence in Sandra's idea. However, there was lingering resistance about the company's financial vulnerability. Noticing this, Sandra realized that she was the only management team member who understood all the project's financial ramifications. To correct this, she asked the accountant to explain precisely what the project meant in dollars and cents. After this explanation, all traces of resistance left and everyone was eager to produce greeting cards. The value they placed on risk taking had also increased.

Sandra recognized that she was successful because she identified and dealt with specific causes of resistance expressed by each management team member. Her methods were a winning combination in modifying values and beliefs that could have interfered with the project's implementation.

In contrast, other people are less resistant to change because they hold values for such things as security, stability, routine, consistency, and dependability. These people are vulnerable to overestimating the risks of change. Their reaction to proposed change is often preceded by the words, "Yes, but . . ." Here are some ways they express their values:

"If it's not broken, why fix it?"

"Our customers count on us for consistency."

"Instead of chasing rainbows, we need to look at the facts."

"This change would send the message that we don't care about our employees."

While values that meet people's needs tend to be stable over time, they aren't immune to change. Morris Massey maintains that once values have been programmed, they can be substantially altered only by what he refers to as *significant emotional events*. Finding out that you have high blood pressure, for example, could be a significant emotional event that causes you to place greater value on your health. Similarly, if you were blamed for declining sales and fired from your job as national sales manager, it is likely that this would be a significant emotional event, causing you to take stock of your life. A change in values at this point could open up new possibilities, leading you in directions you never considered before.

Perhaps the easiest way to see the role of values overcoming resistance to change is to think of the various factors in a cost/benefit analysis. Whereas facts are actual costs and predictive beliefs are anticipated costs, benefits are values. Something is a benefit to people only if it relates to their values. If people want something badly enough, they'll be willing to pay more for it (actual cost) and take more risks to get it (anticipated cost).

Figure 5 shows the interplay of facts, beliefs, and values in a cost/benefit analysis. In scenario #1, low cost and low benefit, the expected reaction would be one of indifference. To bring about change, the perceived benefit would have to be increased to generate any interest. In scenario #2, low cost and high benefit, conditions are favorable to change. In scenario #3, high cost and low benefit, resistance to change can be expected. To overcome resistance to change under these conditions, the perceived benefit would have to be increased to justify the high cost. Finally, in scenario #4, high cost and high benefit, the stage is set for an approach-avoidance conflict. The decision to change would be agonizing,

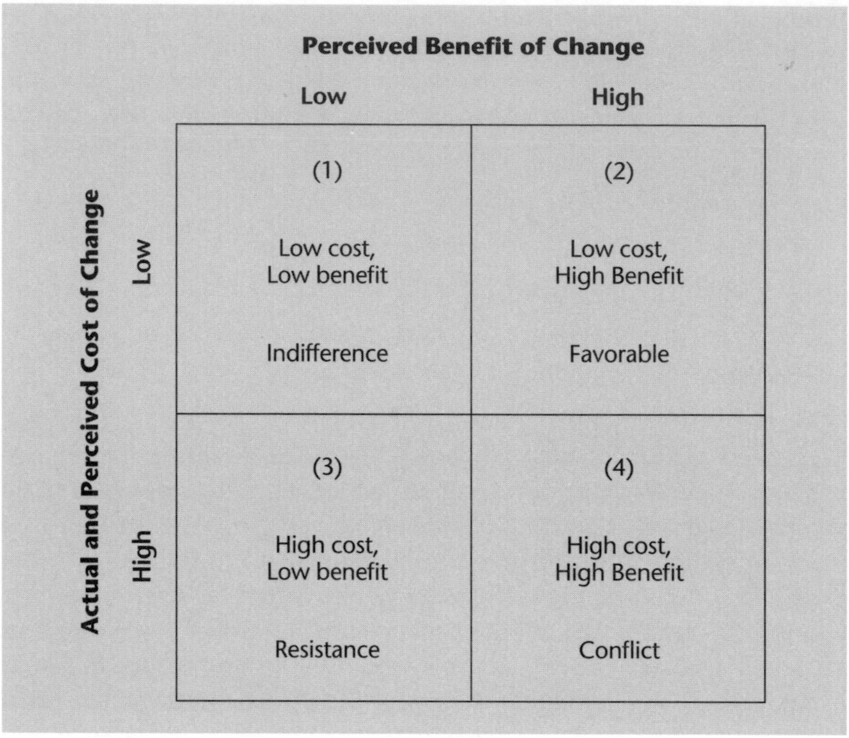

Perceived Benefit of Change

	Low	High
Low	(1) Low cost, Low benefit Indifference	(2) Low cost, High Benefit Favorable
High	(3) High cost, Low benefit Resistance	(4) High cost, High Benefit Conflict

(Vertical axis label: Actual and Perceived Cost of Change)

Figure 5   Cost/Benefit Analysis of Change

as people weigh the high costs against the high benefits. In situations such as this, having access to accurate facts and rational, empirically based beliefs really pays off.

The Role of Behavior

Facts, beliefs, and values help people choose behaviors that allow them to meet their needs. If a behavior is successful at this task, it will tend to be reinforced and to resist change. The facts, beliefs, and values leading up to the behavior will also resist change. If the behavior is unsuccessful, however, the person will be more open to doing something new or different. At the same time, that person may have to consider changing some facts, beliefs, and values. You have to change the way you think before you can change the way you act. When I help organizations overcome resistance to change, I find that the most effective way to help people evaluate their situation is to ask them the following four questions:

1. "What need are you trying to meet?"
2. "Does your behavior meet the need?"
3. "Could the need be met better by doing something new or different?"
4. "What would it take for you to change?"

While these questions—particularly questions three and four—usually generate a lively discussion of facts, beliefs and values, the goal of this process is for people to choose behaviors that enable them to meet their needs.

Reactive Versus Proactive Change

People in organizations can find themselves in two different types of change situations—reactive and proactive. In one sense all change is reactive, because it represents an attempt to meet a need. This way of conceiving change is very narrow, however. For our purposes, it's more useful to think of change in terms of the amount of control people have over the process. Therefore, the word *reactive* will be used to describe situations in which people are required to implement changes made by others or that are imposed on the organization from outside. In these situations people have minimal control, as change is thrust upon them. An example of a change made by others would be a decision to eliminate several layers of supervision and reassign duties to those who remain. An example of change imposed on the organization from the outside would be new safety procedures ordered by a government regulatory agency. These situations are often very upsetting, because those responsible for implementing the change may not have had any input into it, or they may be expected to get others to comply with changes that they don't agree with themselves.

In response to reactive change, people have three options open to them. They can either leave the organization, resist the change, or try to adjust to it. Practical realities, such as house payments and college tuition, often make it impossible for people to leave, and resisting such changes is seldom productive. More often than not, therefore, the only viable option is to adjust to the change. Many reactive situations involve unwanted change, so people will view it as either a real or a perceived loss. If their job is eliminated through downsizing, then the loss is very real. But even if they survive the downsizing, they'll be left to deal with the loss of co-workers. In other instances the loss is less tangible, but no less real. For example, a change could cause people to lose trust in management, lose pride in the organization, or lose the sense that they are valued as employees. They will also be wondering whether or not their own position is safe.

When a change involves loss, real or perceived, people can be expected to go through the five stages of a grief reaction, which are as follows:

Denial. The initial response to an unwanted change is often one of disbelief, dismay, or bewilderment. People are stunned by the change and have trouble believing that it is taking place ("This can't be happening"). The primary feeling in this stage is shock.

Bargaining. Since people perceive the change as a threat, in this stage they tend to rely on escape, avoid, and attack behaviors in a desperate attempt to prevent it from happening. People's objective at this point is damage control, and their primary feeling is fear.

Anger. Once people realize that they're stuck with the change, they experience anger, which may or may not be expressed openly. Anger reflects the helplessness they feel when they're unable to prevent the change from happening.

Depression. Soon people discover that anger isn't accomplishing anything and that they can't reverse the change, so they feel defeated and become depressed. While this stage may appear to lack purpose, this is where people begin making the adjustments in their facts, beliefs, and values that are necessary for them to accept the unwanted change.

Acceptance. As time goes by, people become adjusted to the change and the depression begins to lift. They may never come to like the change, but they learn to live with it.

These five stages represent a natural process of recovery from any loss. Each stage has its proper place and is essential for emotional healing. People can't skip over a step or try to speed up the process. I've always been impressed with how resilient people are in adjusting to reactive change. As people go through this process, the most important thing you can do for them is listen and offer encouragement and support ("I know you're upset, but you've survived worse situations than this. Is there anything I can do to help you?"). Being sensitive to employees during this time of crisis will go a long way toward restoring their confidence in the organization.

Proactive situations are those in which people seek to initiate change and, therefore, have more control over the process. Instead of being forced to change, they're motivated by a desire to do something new or differently. In other words, they are *pursuing* change to accomplish something they believe is important. The amount of control people have to bring about proactive change varies from one situation to the next. People have the most control when it comes to changing themselves and less control when it comes to changing others or an organization.

I define a leader as someone who is willing to assume the risks of change. Initiating change takes courage, especially when opposition is anticipated. One person's proactive change can become someone else's reactive change. Therefore, it's important to have a vision for proactive change and to gain needed support from others. While this process can be challenging, it's often well worth the effort, since proactive change can prevent the need for reactive change later. This book provides concepts and tools that can help overcome resistance to any type of change, but the emphasis is on proactive change.

Summary

Change is difficult, because the outcome is always uncertain. Nevertheless, change is a prerequisite for growth, and it can make the difference between a dull and an exciting life. Sometimes curiosity, boredom, or the desire for a challenge motivate people to change. More often than not, however, external circumstances or problems with meeting important needs require people to venture into new territory. Before they become willing to change, people weigh the costs, relying on facts (actual costs) and beliefs (anticipated costs), and the values, (benefits). Once a decision to change has been made, it is implemented through action. Actions that meet needs will be retained, while actions that don't meet needs will be rejected.

Change can be either reactive or proactive. The ability to navigate change under a wide variety of circumstances is an essential leadership skill, one that can make the difference between success and failure.

Changes in
Organizational Reality

A paradigm is a model accepted by people for explaining the
way something works. A paradigm shift occurs when old facts, beliefs,
values, and behaviors no longer allow people to meet their needs—like
a road map that doesn't get you where you want to go. Throughout his-
tory there have been many paradigm shifts, and there will be others in
the future. The trend toward a global economy represents a current paradigm shift; it is a whole new way of thinking about how business is
conducted. Peter Vaill refers to this as "permanent white water." In
response, all of us are required to make our own personal paradigm
shifts if we hope to be successful in the present economic climate.

Since making even small changes can be traumatic, a paradigm shift
can be experienced as total upheaval. One person described it this way:
"I was going along fine, then someone pressed the fast-forward button."
This is especially difficult for people who have developed a vested interest in their current facts, beliefs, values, and behaviors. They want to
believe their facts are accurate; their beliefs are true, good, and effective
predictors; their values are the best ones; and their behaviors represent
the correct choices. It can be devastating, therefore, when they find out
that their whole way of thinking and acting needs to be revamped.

Talking about a paradigm shift can be a stimulating intellectual exercise, but actually making one is often gut-wrenching—a significant emotional event. When I found myself unemployed shortly after my fiftieth
birthday, I was forced to think about my career from an entirely different
perspective, one that I never anticipated. On several occasions I woke up

in a cold sweat, wondering if I could cope with the ambiguity of my situation. To keep from being overwhelmed by anxiety, I remembered what I told my clients: focus on what you can learn instead of your emotions because learning empowers you to move forward. During that period I learned that uncertainty had become a permanent part of my life, so I had to find ways to thrive in spite of it. I also learned that instead of reinventing my career once, I would have to do it over and over again.

Whether your goal is to keep pace with the new organizational reality yourself or to help other people do this, the following questions, focusing on key components of the motivational cycle, will greatly facilitate this process.

What Is Your Need?

During times of uncertainty or confusion, anxiety often leads people to rush to solutions before being clear about what they want to accomplish. As they talk to me about their struggles, therefore, I find it helpful to ask such questions as, "What is your need?" "What is your objective?" or "What are you trying to accomplish?" This offers them a starting point, so they can think about the issues more rationally and begin developing a systematic plan of action. It also allows them to feel less overwhelmed and more in control of what they're going through. When I was in the midst of my own personal paradigm shift, I reminded myself that what I needed most was a fresh outlook on my career, not just a job. As a result, I was able to focus on the forest, not just the trees.

What Are Your Facts?

A paradigm shift begins with significant changes in facts or objective reality. A good example is what has happened in the world of work during the past two hundred years. We experienced the Agricultural Revolution and then the Industrial Revolution, and now we're in the Information Age. In his book *The End of Affluence,* Jeffrey Madrick points out that during the late 1800s, the service economy accounted for 33 percent of our gross national product. That figure grew to 66 percent after World War II, to 75 percent by the late 1970s, and to over 80 percent today. These changes have brought about a tremendous upheaval in the job market. Thousands upon thousands of adults who thought they were set for life are returning to school for retraining because their current skills are no longer in demand.

Another major trend is the increasing competitiveness of other countries. While the United States essentially controlled the world market until the late 1950s, that is no longer the case. Many other countries now equal or surpass us in terms of productivity, cost, and quality. For example, in the 1960s East Asia accounted for only 4 percent of the world's economic output, but now it accounts for more than 25 percent. In 1950, the United States produced 76 percent of all motor vehicles, but in 1994 it produced only 25 percent. In an effort to remain competitive, U.S. firms have had to make major changes in quality and efficiency.

When preparing for change, whether personal or organizational, the first step is to gather up-to-date information that is accurate, complete, and free from distortion. As we go through the motivational cycle, everything else that happens depends on this. Inaccurate, incomplete, or distorted information is not only useless, but it can be harmful.

What Are Your Beliefs?

In Chapter 3, I indicated that beliefs are more important than facts, because they represent the meanings attached to factual information. By themselves facts don't serve as motives, but the meanings people attach to facts can be powerful motives. Since beliefs are subjective variables and not objective realities, their usefulness doesn't depend on whether they're popular but on whether they're *viable* (workable, helpful, useful). Beliefs should be evaluated by their results, not by how good or bad they may sound. Viable beliefs will be accurately grounded on facts, making them empirically based, while nonviable beliefs will lack empirical evidence.

In evaluating the viability of specific beliefs, some useful questions to ask are these:

"What proof do you have?"

"What other factors should we consider?"

"Could these facts be explained in any other way?"

"Should we gather more information before going with this conclusion?"

"Do your beliefs allow you to meet your needs? If not, then what good are they? Why fight to keep them?"

Table 3

Viable/Unviable Beliefs About Yourself

Unviable	Viable
I wouldn't be able to survive if I lost my job.	If I lost my job, I could use my knowledge and skills elsewhere.
I can take the safe way.	There is no safe way.
The change won't impact me.	The change will impact everyone.
I've worked hard to get where I am, and I deserve this job.	If I try to rest on yesterday's laurels I'll fall behind.
The organization is responsible for my security.	I'm responsible for my own security.
Once I'm secure I can be creative.	Security is the enemy of creativity.
It's dangerous to take risks.	It's dangerous to keep doing things the old way.
I know my job well enough already; I don't need to grow.	Grow or die.
I can hang on until I retire.	If I just try to hang on, I'll stifle myself and the organization.
I better not admit to mistakes; it might get me in trouble.	I must take responsibility for mistakes and try to learn from them.
All I need to know is my own job.	I need to know about a lot of jobs.

Tables 3, 4, and 5 provide some examples of viable and unviable beliefs about self, others, and the organization in the present economic climate. Notice that in almost every instance the viable and unviable beliefs are the exact opposites of each other. Viable beliefs emphasize taking responsibility for oneself; facing reality directly; diversifying one's knowledge, skills, and experience; seeking opportunities in the midst of uncertainty; building relationships based on trust, cooperation, and mutual respect; placing the needs of the customer first; taking risks rather than taking orders; and being a leader rather than a follower. Security no longer resides in what others can give us, but in what we can do.

Many people fall by the wayside because, in spite of their best efforts, they aren't capable of making the necessary changes, and many others don't want to make changes and resist them. I served as a consultant for one organization in which managers were deciding whether or not to keep people based on their beliefs about who could and could not

Table 4

Viable/Unviable Beliefs About Other People

Unviable	Viable
I don't need other people, I can depend on myself.	We need to depend on each other to beat the competition.
Individuals are usually more creative than teams.	Teams are usually more creative than individuals.
The best ideas come from management.	Good ideas can come from anywhere in the organization.
Don't trust co-workers; they might be after your job.	You have to trust co-workers to focus on the competition.
You need power and control to get people to do their work.	Power and control inhibit creativity and cause resentment.
Sharing information gives others power over you.	Sharing information is necessary to achieve mutual goals.
You have to protect your own turf.	While you're protecting your turf, the competition is gaining on you.
Managers should be bosses.	Managers should be coaches.

embrace the team concept. At another organization, a key manager quit because he didn't want to share control with a team. In my opinion, among the total workforce only a small percentage will come to embrace the current, viable beliefs and find creative ways to thrive within the present conditions. One of the primary purposes of this book is to help increase that percentage. It's important to remember, however, that while certain beliefs may be viable now, they may not be viable in the future (many of the unviable beliefs listed in the tables were once viable). The key is to continually seek new information and then update your beliefs to reflect that information.

What Are Your Feelings?

Empirically based, rational beliefs tend to produce positive feelings, while non-empirically based, irrational beliefs tend to produce negative feelings. Whenever people experience negative feelings, therefore, they should review their facts and the beliefs stemming from those

Table 5

Viable/Unviable Beliefs About the Organization

Unviable	Viable
We can remain the same and survive.	We need to change to survive.
Things will remain the same or change slowly.	Things will never be the same, and change will be rapid.
The organization will always be here.	The organization must remain competitive to survive.
Security is in the organization.	Security is in your knowledge, skills, and experience.
People with seniority will be protected.	People need to add value, not just put in time.
Conformity is the key to success.	Versatility is the key to success.
The organization owes me for my service.	The organization pays me for my service.
The organization will look out for my interests.	The organization will look out for its own interests.
We work for the organization.	We work for the customer; the organization is where the work is done.
I've done my job; if customers don't like it that's their problem.	My job isn't complete until the customer is satisfied.
Communication works best top-down.	Any barrier to communication is harmful.
Our products/services are already good enough.	Our products/services can be offered faster, cheaper, and better by someone else.

facts, ridding themselves of the ones that don't stand up under scrutiny. At the same time, remember that anxiety, while usually considered a negative feeling, isn't always bad and even can be a positive source of motivation. Anxiety stemming from mistaken, inaccurate, or distorted facts and beliefs is almost always harmful, but it is unrealistic to expect people to make major changes without being anxious because they will be acutely aware of their vulnerability.

Remember that desire to succeed and fear of failure go hand in hand. If you didn't care about being successful, then you wouldn't worry about failure. Accordingly, I view self-confidence not as the absence of anxiety, but rather as action in the face of anxiety. Self-confidence is facing reality as it is, even though some aspects of it might be troublesome. People either can try something new in spite of their anxiety or avoid it because of anxiety. Unfortunately, the world will not wait for those in the latter category to catch up and will simply leave them behind. When I was experiencing my own paradigm shift I experienced a great deal of anxiety, but I knew I still had to move forward. Doing this increased my self-confidence, but the anxiety never disappeared completely.

What Are Your Values?

Values are the criteria we use for making decisions. People develop a vested interest in the particular values they embrace, and they want to believe that their values are the best ones or even the only ones. Since values are subjective variables, however, they can't be proven right or wrong. A misconception people have is that values are entirely benevolent and positive aspects of personality. Unfortunately, values can lead to very destructive and negative results. The highest achievements of human beings have been motivated by values, but so have wars, discrimination, hate, crime, riots, and other malevolent human behavior. As with beliefs, therefore, values should be evaluated on their viability.

Some values will be more useful than others in the current economic climate. Table 6 lists viable and unviable work values. Although many of the values in the unviable column were viable in the past, they have been replaced by values that are their opposites. Gone are the days when lone rangers stacked on top of each other in elaborate hierarchies demand loyalty, control information, and bark out commands to achieve goals. Today's organizations are flatter and leaner, allowing for greater speed, flexibility, and responsiveness. Also gone are the consumers who bought something and felt grateful if it worked. Now consumers are empowered; they demand quality for a reasonable price and take their business elsewhere if they don't get it. Consequently, quality, trust, accountability, team performance, networking, risk taking, empowerment, process improvement, and leadership are values necessary for survival.

Many people will have trouble making the kinds of changes that are needed. The adjustments required will take them way out of their comfort zones. Nevertheless, perseverance, determination, and a willingness to ask for help and to obtain additional training will augur well for eventual success.

Table 6

Viable and Unviable Work Values

Unviable	Viable
Productivity	Quality
Security	Risk taking/courage
Tenure/seniority	Adding value
Conformity	Innovativeness
Predictability	Flexibility
Control	Empowerment
Independence/dependence	Interdependence
Individual contribution	Team contribution
Internal competition	Cooperation
Personal success	Customer success
Outcome focus	Process focus
Reactive	Proactive
Expediency	Integrity
Formality	Informality
Following procedures	Responsiveness
Privilege/special interests	Inclusiveness
Clear boundaries	Boundarylessness
Similarity	Diversity
Traditional education	Lifelong learning
Management	Leadership
Tactical	Strategic
Meeting standards	Continuous improvement

Empirically based, rational beliefs and the positive feelings they produce foster values that enable people to pursue meaningful goals, while non-empirically based, irrational beliefs and the negative feelings they produce foster values designed to protect people from perceived danger. Values in the former category tend to be proactive and empowering, while those in the latter category tend to be reactive and defensive. Even the casual observer of organizational behavior will be aware of the constant ebb and flow of people's desire to accomplish something and their need to protect themselves.

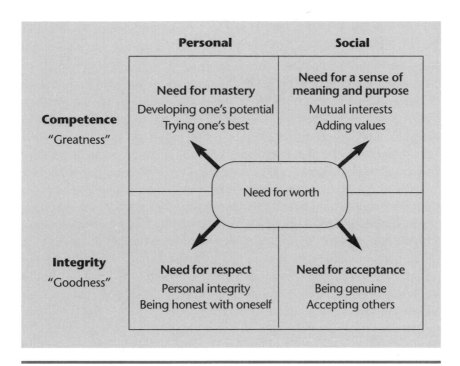

Figure 6   Relationship Between Needs and Values

As a counselor, consultant, and trainer, one of my objectives is to help people increase the amount of time they spend trying to make good things happen and to decrease the amount of time they spend trying to prevent bad things from happening. I challenge them to identify inaccurate facts and unviable beliefs that give rise to fear and to exchange them for accurate facts and viable, confidence-producing beliefs. At the same time, I encourage them to embrace proactive values that will help them achieve their goals.

In Chapter 2, I indicated that our deepest psychological need is to view ourselves and be viewed by others as having worth as a person, and that we endeavor to accomplish this by striving to meet four subneeds: mastery, a sense of meaning and purpose, respect, and acceptance. In my opinion, there are eight values that are especially viable ways to pursue these subneeds in the current business climate, two pertaining to each need. Because of their power to serve as a catalyst for success, I refer to them as *megavalues*. The relationship between the four subneeds and eight megavalues is shown in Figure 6.

Developing One's Potential
Versus Preserving the Status Quo

Some of the most gut-wrenching consulting I've done has been with large organizations in the midst of downsizing their middle manager ranks. Both the managers who are fired and the ones remaining face major challenges. Those in the former category feel hurt, angry, and betrayed, since many of them believed acceptable performance guaranteed them a job for life. They're also faced with considerable anxiety and uncertainty about their future. Those in the latter category feel angry that their colleagues and friends were severed, guilty yet relieved that they still have a job, and worried about how long that job will last.

The managers in both groups who make the best adjustment are those who place a value on developing their potential, as opposed to preserving the status quo. Among those who lose their jobs, many who cling to the past simply disappear from the workforce, unable to cope with the thought of looking for a new job or going back to school, while those who believe they still have potential either seek opportunities in the same field or begin retraining for another one. In retrospect, some who choose to develop themselves are actually grateful for having been laid off, because they are forced to make choices that result in career enhancement.

Managers surviving a downsizing realize that preserving the status quo is the kiss of death; they'll be required to expand their knowledge and skills if they plan to have a future with the organization. Many of them develop greater self-confidence and eventually become more effective contributors, as they take the initiative to participate in educational programs.

The world of work will continue to experience rapid and unpredictable change. While people won't have very much control over the nature of that change, and job security is a thing of the past, people do have control over developing their potential. By learning and growing, they increase their chances of remaining viable, whether it's with their current organization or in some other endeavor. Fulfilling their need for mastery is therefore one of the best ways people can empower themselves.

Doing One's Best Versus Trying to Be Perfect

Perfectionism is one of the ten inner obstacles Bernstein and Rozen describe in their book *Sacred Bull*. People who strive for perfection worry about whether they have done enough or have made a mistake, putting pressure on both themselves and those around them. Compulsively seeking improvement, perfectionists tend to micromanage people, sending the message that they lack confidence in others. They fill the work environment with pressure and tension, as others feel that their work is constantly under scrutiny.

Trying to be perfect isn't viable because people don't have control over all the factors affecting performance. No matter how hard people strive to dot every *i* and cross every *t,* something always seems to happen to upset the best laid plans. In contrast, trying their best is within people's control and, therefore, much more viable. Whereas fear of making mistakes keeps perfectionists from being able to enjoy their work, people who try their best can relax and find pleasure in using their talents and abilities. Even if something doesn't work out, they can know they did all they could instead of wonder if they could or should have done more. This frame of mind also allows them to be a source of support and encouragement to others in the workplace.

Concern for Mutual Interests Versus Concern for Self-Interest

People can be divided into two camps: those who show concern for others and those who are concerned only for themselves. Co-workers heap accolades on the former, saying, "He's a team player," "Whenever I ask her for help, she always goes the extra mile," or "He puts the interests of others above his own." On the latter, co-workers heap disdain, saying, "The only one she cares about is herself," "He'll only help you if there's something in it for him," or "Never turn your back on him; he'll walk all over you to get ahead." Obviously, people are much more likely to trust those concerned about mutual interests than those concerned about self-interest. Although we don't have control over whether people look out for our interests, we can still choose to look out for their interests.

A team never becomes cohesive if members perceive each other as only looking out for themselves or if they believe they can accomplish their goals without each other. Only when team members show genuine concern for each other and have a sense of interdependence are they able to flourish. Working with others toward common goals helps people meet their need for a sense of meaning and purpose. People tend to focus on self-interest when they don't trust others to take their needs into consideration. Making it clear that people are expected to work together toward mutual interests can help them build a greater level of trust.

Adding Value Versus Seeking Recognition

People seeking recognition try to draw attention to their work and take credit for success, while people seeking to add value focus on making a contribution and sharing success. Co-workers avoid those who toot their own horn but gravitate toward those willing to be team players.

One of the best ways to add value in an organization is by listening. "Seek first to understand, then to be understood," is one of the habits Stephen Covey discusses in his book *The Seven Habits of Highly Effective People*. People have a deep need to be understood. Feeling understood allows people to feel less isolated and instills in them a sense of hope when they're discouraged. People have often made comments to me such as, "Thanks for listening," "I don't feel so alone anymore," "I feel so much better now," and "I've gained a fresh perspective on my situation just because you let me talk about it." This, in turn, has allowed me to feel that I've contributed something to other people, helping me to meet my need for a sense of meaning and purpose. While people don't have control over whether others listen to them, they do have control over listening to others.

Unfortunately, people seldom trust others to listen. It's commonplace to hear remarks like, "No one listens to me," "No one understands me," or "No one cares what I think." When people feel this way, they tend to either remain silent or talk more in an effort to be understood. I've facilitated team meetings where everyone was clamoring for attention and no one was listening. Voices would increase in volume as people competed for air time. When this happens, I like to call a time out and ask, "Does anyone here feel understood?" This rhetorical question forces team members to step back and examine their pattern of interaction and to establish norms requiring people to listen and convey understanding before expressing their own views. When people begin trusting others to listen, this frees them up to listen in return.

Personal Integrity Versus Expediency

Integrity is a subject of increasing interest in the professional literature, as evidenced by the publication of such books as *The Power of Ethical Management* by Ken Blanchard and Norman Vincent Peale and *Leadership and the Quest for Integrity* by Joseph Badaracco Jr. and Richard Ellsworth. People want to view themselves and to be viewed by others as being moral and ethical. An unwritten code of ethics exists between people. As they deal with each other, they have a sense for what's right and wrong. We refer to this as "common sense." While people don't always have control over the circumstances, they can still decide to do what they believe is right. People who act out of integrity inspire confidence and trust, helping them meet their need for respect. People who act out of expediency, however, inspire suspicion and doubt. They often rationalize their actions in order to maintain their self-esteem, creating even more suspicion.

While some people are unscrupulous and try to take advantage of others, in my experience most people choose expediency over integrity in response to a perceived danger, real or imagined. Helping them identify and deal with the danger can create the conditions necessary for them to restore their integrity. This not only allows them to feel better about themselves, but also allows other people to feel better about them.

Being Honest with Oneself Versus Seeking Self-Justification

Some people have a strong enough sense of self-worth to be honest with themselves about their strengths and weaknesses, while others attempt to maintain self-worth by avoiding anything that might reflect on them negatively. Those in the former category take responsibility for their actions, regarding corrective feedback as an opportunity to increase their effectiveness. This type of honesty can help people develop their potential. Those in the latter category, however, externalize responsibility for their actions. Corrective feedback is viewed as threatening, so they tend to respond to it defensively. When confronted with a problem, therefore, they deny, rationalize, minimize, or blame others. Since they don't learn from their mistakes, they're doomed to repeat them.

In addition to fostering personal and career growth, being honest with oneself allows people to serve as good role models for others seeking to learn effective organizational behaviors. When those in leadership positions take responsibility for their mistakes and seek corrective feedback from others, including subordinates, it removes fear from relationships and revolutionizes the performance appraisal process. This is one of the best ways to act on Deming's management principle *drive out fear*. While being honest with oneself takes courage, it provides others with an example worthy of emulation.

Being Genuine Versus Posturing

One of people's deepest desires is to be authentic or real with others and to have others be real with them. This helps them meet their need for acceptance. While people crave this kind of openness, fear of being rejected, humiliated, or embarrassed makes it a rarity in organizational life. In fact, after having worked with thousands of people in many organizations for more than thirty years, I estimate that about 80 percent of the interaction between people represents posturing—the dynamics are tainted by hidden agendas—while only about 20 percent is genuine. How many times have you sat through a meeting where two people were having a very diplomatic exchange, only to have one of them tell you later what he or she *really* thinks. Even during these moments of candor, however, it's difficult to tell if the person is being honest with you or has a hidden agenda. This sort of drama takes place every day in every organization.

People are often skeptical that others are being genuine with them, so they play their cards close to the chest, being genuine only after determining that it's safe. Since it's difficult to tell if it really is safe, however, people tend to err on the side of posturing. They wait to see if others are authentic before being authentic themselves, but this means everyone wastes a lot of time waiting. It takes courage to let your guard down when you are unsure how others will respond, but this is more viable than spending eight hours a day pretending to be someone you aren't. Genuineness is infectious; if you take the initiative to be yourself, it frees others up to be themselves. This helps to create a healthier interpersonal environment in the workplace.

Accepting Others Versus Judging Others

People want to believe that they're okay as they are now, not that they have to change in order to be okay. This helps them meet their need for acceptance, which is essential for the development of a cohesive team. Whenever people enter a new job situation they're asking themselves such questions as, "What are the ground rules here?" "How are people expected to act?" "What goes and what doesn't?" During their first several months of employment—the honeymoon period—most people make an effort to fit in, but they're also looking for a way to express their individuality and uniqueness. The tension between conformity and individuality can have a powerful effect on employee morale. Over the years, I've heard many people say such things as, "They expect us to act like robots," "I can't be myself around here," "I've got to get out of this place; it's too stifling for me."

When people feel insecure they tend to act the way they think others want them to act, keeping their individuality hidden. What they say and do becomes very stilted, as they continually try to please others. The problem with this is that we can't control the acceptance others offer us; we can control only the acceptance we offer them. The best way to receive acceptance is to give it.

A related issue is prejudice in the workplace. People want to be judged by their work performance, not by external characteristics such as race, gender,

Table 7

Pursuing Viable Values Gives You Control

Megavalue Choices	Your Area of Control
Developing One's Potential Versus Preserving the Status Quo	You have control over whether you seek out learning opportunities.
Doing One's Best Versus Trying to Be Perfect	You have control over using your talents and abilities to the fullest.
Concern for Mutual Interests Versus Concern for Self-Interest	You have control over whether you're willing to give to others.
Adding Value Versus Seeking Recognition	You have control over contributing to the common good.
Personal Integrity Versus Expediency	You have control over showing others you can be trusted.
Being Honest with Oneself Versus Seeking Self-Justification	You have control over whether you're honest with yourself.
Being Genuine Versus Posturing	You have control over whether you're honest with others.
Accepting Others Versus Judging Others	You have control over whether you accept people for who they are.

age, ethnicity, religion, lifestyle, or socioeconomic class. Showing respect for differences allows people to feel like they belong. In contrast, discrimination creates a hostile work environment. People tend to be judgmental when they lack understanding of differences or feel threatened by them.

Unfortunately, it's unrealistic to expect that we can eradicate prejudice, since people's attitudes toward differences are often deeply ingrained. We can, however, make it clear that there's no place for discrimination in the organization. Also, we can encourage training programs designed to increase understanding of differences, and we can behave in ways that demonstrate a commitment to fostering diversity and inclusiveness.

A summary of the eight megavalues, emphasizing the areas over which you have control, is provided in Table 7.

What Are Your Behaviors?

While accurate facts and viable beliefs and values are prerequisites to effective behaviors, they aren't sufficient, because many behaviors require a high level of knowledge and skill. If people lack the necessary

Table 8

Effective and Ineffective Behaviors

Ineffective	Effective
Staying with the familiar	Exploring new possibilities
Deferring to authority	Assertiveness
Talking	Listening
Pointing the finger, passing the blame	Taking responsibility for one's actions
Manipulating	Dealing with issues directly
Withholding information	Sharing information
Protecting turf	Networking
Gaining and keeping power	Sharing power
Doing the minimum to get by	Doing whatever it takes
Discriminating against others	Respecting differences
Focusing on self-interests	Focusing on mutual interests
Holding others back	Encouraging others
Following orders	Taking the initiative
Seeking win-lose outcomes	Seeking win-win outcomes

knowledge and skills, therefore, they must be willing to obtain additional education and training. This is crucial, because organizations evaluate people not on their beliefs and values but on their actions. Table 8 offers a summary of the behaviors required for people to be effective in today's organizations. As you can see, these behaviors are consistent with the viable beliefs and values already discussed.

Is Your Need Met?

The bottom line for everything discussed in this chapter can be summarized by this question: Did you meet your need or didn't you? If so, you can go on to your next need. If not, you'll have to go back through the motivational cycle; reexamine your facts, beliefs, values, and behaviors, and be prepared to make the changes required to meet your need. Having the courage to confront and change your thoughts, feelings, decisions, and behaviors will increase your chances of being successful, and it will give you the credibility required to lead others through change.

Understanding Values

Purpose

The purposes of this exercise are to help people understand more fully how their own values developed and to gain a greater appreciation for the values of others. It can serve as an excellent way to foster team building. The exercise is designed to take one hour.

Procedures for Group Use

1. Divide participants into groups of four to six.

2. Cover the following points:

> According to Dr. Morris Massey, about 90 percent of our values are programmed by our surroundings by the time we are ten years old. He maintains that once values have been programmed, only significant emotional events can substantially alter them.

> Each generation develops and programs a set of values, which people then try to impose on others. When individuals from one value system attempt to manage individuals from another, it often results in conflict.

3. Hand out a copy of the page entitled "How You Became Who You Are" to each participant. It summarizes some of the significant emotional events for various current age groups that took place when they were about ten years old. Cover these points:

> When individuals from one value system try to manage individuals from another, it often results in conflict.

> Everyone wants to believe their values are the right ones or the best ones. As a result, people often have difficulty relating to others with different values.

> We need to find ways to build bridges between people with different values, so there can be more cooperation in the workplace.

4. Hand out a copy of the page entitled "Your Values" to each participant and give these instructions:

> Take a few minutes to complete "Your Values" individually.

> Then take turns sharing with other members of your group whatever information you would like about the events that have shaped your life.

5. Debrief key learning points with the full group by asking these questions:

> What did you learn about yourself and other people in your group?

> How similar or different are the values of individuals in your group?

> What are some of the similarities and differences?

> In what ways are the things you've learned about each other relevant to your day-to-day working relationship?

6. Ask for and respond to questions.

Procedures for Individual Use

1. Read the page entitled "How You Became Who You Are" and find the category that matches your current age.

2. Answer the questions on the "Your Values" page and spend some time thinking about how the events in your life have affected your values.

How You Became Who You Are

Current Age	When Value Programmed
70s	**1930s**

Depression
Security
Small towns
Family farms

60s	**1940s**

World War II
National pride
Family fragmentation
Mobility

50s	**1950s**

Korean War
Indulged kids
Dr. Spock
Television
Affluence ("The American Dream")
Baby boomers

40s	**1960s**

Space program
Civil rights
Kennedys
Vietnam War
Hippies (idealists)

30s	**1970s**

Jet Age
Credit cards
Computers
Watergate
Yuppies (money-oriented)

20s	**1980s**

Immediate gratification
Job-Hopping
Videotapes
Cellular phones
Generation X

Your Values

What circumstances or events shaped your values when you were a child?

In what ways have your values changed since you became an adult, and what significant emotional events caused those changes?

The Megavalue Scale

Purpose

The Megavalue Scale and Plan for Personal Change are designed to give people an opportunity to take stock of their current values, beliefs, and behaviors, and to decide what changes they want to make. Both exercises assume that people are familiar with the material presented in this chapter. The Megavalue Scale takes thirty minutes to complete, while the Plan for Personal Change takes one hour.

Procedures for Group Use

1. Explain that participants will now have an opportunity to assess their current values.
2. Hand out a copy of the Megavalue Scale to each participant, including the instrument itself, scoring instruction sheet, and Megavalue Profile.
3. Give instructions for completing the instrument, calculating scores, and plotting the Profile.
4. After everyone has completed the Megavalue Profile, explain how to interpret the results: The higher your scores, the more viable your values in the current business climate. Low scores reveal areas where improvement is needed.
5. Ask for comments and reactions.

Procedures for Individual Use

1. Follow the directions below.
2. After completing the Megavalue Profile, spend some time thinking about the results, noting areas of strength and areas where improvement is indicated.

Directions

The Megavalue Scale is designed to assess the degree to which your decisions are motivated by values that are viable in the current business climate. First read each item and circle the response that best applies to you. Next calculate your scores, and then complete the Megavalue Profile.

These are tough questions requiring careful thought and reflection. As you answer them, please be honest with yourself; otherwise the results will be meaningless. This is feedback for yourself only. You won't be required to share the information with anyone else.

In my daily work I

1. Avoid trying new things	4	3	2	1	0
2. Strive to be perfect	4	3	2	1	0
3. Keep information to myself	4	3	2	1	0
4. Draw attention to my work	4	3	2	1	0
5. Compromise what I believe is right to stay out of trouble	4	3	2	1	0
6. Avoid thinking about things that make me feel bad about myself	4	3	2	1	0
7. Pretend to agree with others	4	3	2	1	0
8. Evaluate people on the basis of external characteristics	4	3	2	1	0
9. Prefer using my current skills to developing new ones	4	3	2	1	0
10. Get frustrated if I can't do something right	4	3	2	1	0
11. Focus on getting what I want	4	3	2	1	0
12. Try to impress others	4	3	2	1	0
13. Bend the truth if necessary to protect myself	4	3	2	1	0
14. Make excuses for myself	4	3	2	1	0
15. Talk about people behind their backs	4	3	2	1	0
16. Feel uneasy around people different from me	4	3	2	1	0
17. Fail to take advantage of learning opportunities	4	3	2	1	0
18. Put myself down when I make a mistake	4	3	2	1	0
19. Share information when it's to my advantage	4	3	2	1	0
20. Try to compete with co-workers	4	3	2	1	0
21. Let the end justify the means	4	3	2	1	0
22. Blame others or circumstances when something goes wrong	4	3	2	1	0
23. Tell people what I think they want to hear	4	3	2	1	0

In my daily work I

24. Avoid people who are different from me	4	3	2	1	0
25. Resist change	4	3	2	1	0
26. Focus on what I do wrong rather than on what I do right	4	3	2	1	0
27. Look out for my own interests	4	3	2	1	0
28. Seek recognition for my work	4	3	2	1	0
29. Cut corners to get the job done	4	3	2	1	0
30. Minimize my mistakes	4	3	2	1	0
31. Keep my real thoughts and feelings to myself	4	3	2	1	0
32. Regard people different from me less favorably	4	3	2	1	0
33. Try to get by on what I know already	4	3	2	1	0
34. Blow small mistakes out of proportion	4	3	2	1	0
35. Offer help when I have something to gain	4	3	2	1	0
36. Prefer giving my views instead of listening to the views of others	4	3	2	1	0
37. Look for ways to get around the rules	4	3	2	1	0
38. Deny my shortcomings	4	3	2	1	0
39. Choose what I say very carefully	4	3	2	1	0
40. Prefer to be around people holding similar views	4	3	2	1	0

Calculating Your Scores

This instrument consists of eight value choices with five items for each. To develop your own Megavalue Profile:

1. On the worksheet below, total the scores you gave yourself for the five items pertaining to each value choice.
2. Place a dot at the corresponding point on the continuum on page 89 for each value on the Megavalue Profile.
3. Connect the dots with a line.

Developing One's Potential	Doing One's Best	Concern for Mutual Interests	Adding Value
1 _____	2 _____	3 _____	4 _____
9 _____	10 _____	11 _____	12 _____
17 _____	18 _____	19 _____	20 _____
25 _____	26 _____	27 _____	28 _____
33 _____	34 _____	35 _____	36 _____
TOTAL _____	TOTAL _____	TOTAL _____	TOTAL _____

Personal Integrity	Being Honest with Oneself	Being Genuine	Accepting Others
5 _____	6 _____	7 _____	8 _____
13 _____	14 _____	15 _____	16 _____
21 _____	22 _____	23 _____	24 _____
29 _____	30 _____	31 _____	32 _____
37 _____	38 _____	39 _____	40 _____
TOTAL _____	TOTAL _____	TOTAL _____	TOTAL _____

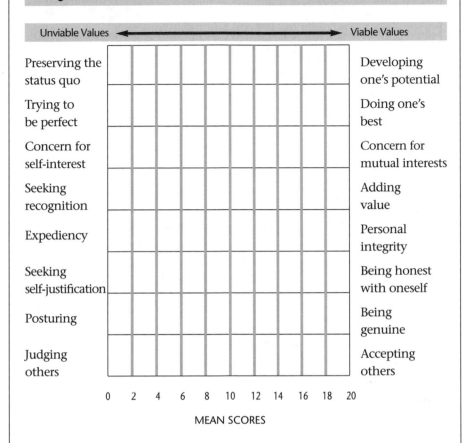

Megavalue Profile

| Unviable Values ← | | | | | | | | | | → Viable Values |

Preserving the status quo											Developing one's potential
Trying to be perfect											Doing one's best
Concern for self-interest											Concern for mutual interests
Seeking recognition											Adding value
Expediency											Personal integrity
Seeking self-justification											Being honest with oneself
Posturing											Being genuine
Judging others											Accepting others

0 2 4 6 8 10 12 14 16 18 20

MEAN SCORES

By examining the profile, you can see which of your values are more viable than others. High scores reveal areas of strength, while low scores reveal areas where improvement is needed.

Plan for Personal Change

Procedures for Group Use
1. Explain the purpose for the Plan for Personal Change:

    You will now have a chance to pull together what you've learned about viable/unviable beliefs and values, effective/ineffective behaviors, and your current values, and decide what changes you want to make to foster your personal growth.

2. Hand out the two-page Plan for Personal Change, and give instructions for completing it:

    Individually, identify values you'd like to emphasize more fully, unviable beliefs you'd like to change, more viable beliefs you can substitute for the unviable ones, and new behaviors you plan to try out in support of your viable beliefs and values.

    Take about fifteen minutes to do this.

3. Divide participants into groups of four to six and give the following instructions:

    Now take turns sharing your plan with the others in your group, seeking their feedback and suggestions.

    You will have forty-five minutes for this discussion.

4. Debrief key learning points with the whole group:

    What did you get out of this exercise?

    How did your teammates help you make decisions about what to do differently?

    What were the most helpful suggestions you received?

    Any aha's?

Procedures for Individual Use
1. Review the questions on the two-page Plan for Personal Change.
2. Considering what you've learned about yourself from reading this chapter, identify values you'd like to emphasize more fully, unviable beliefs you'd like to change, more viable beliefs you can substitute for the unviable ones, and new behaviors you can try out in support of your viable beliefs and values.

Plan for Personal Change

1. Identify values you'd like to emphasize more fully.

2. Identify unviable beliefs you'd like to change.

3. Identify more viable beliefs you can substitute for unviable ones.

4. Identify new behaviors you plan to try out in support of your viable beliefs and values.

Diagnosing and Overcoming Resistance to Change

Many attempts to deal with resistance to organizational change are doomed to failure because people react to symptoms instead of causes, or they use a shotgun approach, responding to vastly different types of resistance in the same way. Building on the conceptual framework presented in Part 1, Part 2 is intended to help you develop your knowledge and skills in diagnosing and overcoming resistance.

Chapter 6, Assessing Resistance, defines resistance and contrasts it with readiness to change. Not all resistance is bad, and not all change is good. This chapter explains some conditions under which change should be resisted. In addition, it discusses the symptoms of resistance and describes some of the problems associated with diagnosing causes of resistance.

Diagnosing resistance is like putting together a puzzle. Chapter 7, Locating Causes of Resistance, presents the resistance matrix, a model that can be used to piece together a diagnosis by observing what people say and do. The goal is to help you become a "behavioral detective," capable of identifying the information necessary to zero in on a diagnosis.

Chapter 8, Diagnosing Causes of Resistance, helps you synthesize the information you've gathered through your observations of people's behavior to formulate an accurate diagnosis. Information in this chapter will help you diagnose both typical and atypical causes of resistance.

Lack of trust is such a common cause of resistance to organizational change that Chapter 9, Building Trust, is devoted entirely to this topic. Materials are included at the end for conducting a workshop on building trust. The Trust Scale identifies specific behaviors responsible for mistrust, while the Plan for Building Trust helps a team agree on methods for developing greater trust.

Chapter 10, Strategies for Overcoming Resistance, presents the Resistance Strategy Model, which can be used to develop and implement strategies for overcoming resistance. The Resistance Strategy Model is a culmination of everything discussed in the book—it tells how to deal with the underlying causes of resistance and not simply the symptoms; it presents specific strategies for dealing with the eight common causes of resistance; and it shows when and where to use the four inventories and eight exercises in this book with the members in the organization who are involved in the organizational change effort. Finally, drawing on the concepts and exercises presented in the previous nine chapters, the Change Planning Guide allows people to formulate a plan of action for implementing change, which can offset resistance from the beginning.

6

Assessing Resistance

Perhaps the best way to begin our discussion of resistance is to compare it with readiness. *Readiness* is a state of mind that reflects receptivity or even a willingness to change the ways we think and behave, whereas *resistance* reflects unwillingness or unreceptiveness. Readiness is manifested in either active initiation of change or cooperation with it. In contrast, resistance is manifested in either active opposition to change or an attempt to escape or avoid it. Resistance occurs at the moment when fear overtakes desire as our dominant motive. In conversations, people frequently use the term *resistance* to refer to a particular behavior. There's nothing wrong with this as long as we remember that resistance begins as a state of mind.

Readiness is not the opposite of resistance, since an absence of resistance doesn't necessarily mean a readiness to change. Other factors, such as lack of information or an immediate need to attend to other matters, could interfere with readiness. Nevertheless, anything that causes resistance can be expected to undermine readiness.

Why do people resist change? Life is the proving ground for beliefs, values, and behaviors. Those beliefs, values, and behaviors that are successful at meeting our needs will be retained, while those that are unsuccessful will be modified or discarded. Those that initially serve as effective guides to need fulfillment tend to influence the establishment of subsequent beliefs, values, and behaviors, which function much like a fraternity. New beliefs, values, and behaviors are admitted only if they are perceived as being compatible with existing members. In this way the personality of an individual evolves.

Any belief, value, or behavior that has been successful in meeting needs will resist change. Those that have been consistently reinforced through experience and that serve as the core around which other beliefs, values, and behaviors are added will be the most resistant to change, whereas those that are less reliable in meeting needs will be more amenable to change. The degree of personal investment is greater for the former than for the latter. People develop such a strong commitment to their most reliable beliefs, values, and behaviors that it's difficult for them to think of themselves apart from them. They and their beliefs, values, and behaviors become synonymous.

When people perceive that an established belief, value, or behavior is threatened, they experience fear, which then motivates them to protect and defend themselves. The intensity of the fear can vary from mild to extreme, depending on the importance attached to a particular belief, value, or behavior. The more fear there is, the more resistance there will be.

To understand resistance we must also look at the relationships among beliefs, values, and behaviors. Changing one component will have an impact on the others. For example, if people learn to do something they believed was beyond their capabilities, they will most likely change what they believe they can do and also what they want to do (value). Therefore, while it may appear to be simple enough for a person to change one belief, value, or behavior, related beliefs, values, and behaviors could complicate this change or even prevent it from happening.

Willingness Versus Ability to Change

It's important to make a distinction between resistance to change and inability to change. Whereas resistance represents unwillingness or unreceptiveness, inability to change stems from lack of knowledge, skills, confidence, and/or necessary resources. Knowledge and skills have to do with one's actual ability, whereas confidence has to do with one's perceived ability. Resources can be divided into two categories: working conditions and communication. Working conditions are largely concerned with the availability and allocation of staff, money, time, equipment, and supplies; communication has to do with the interpersonal environment on the job, and concerns such things as the

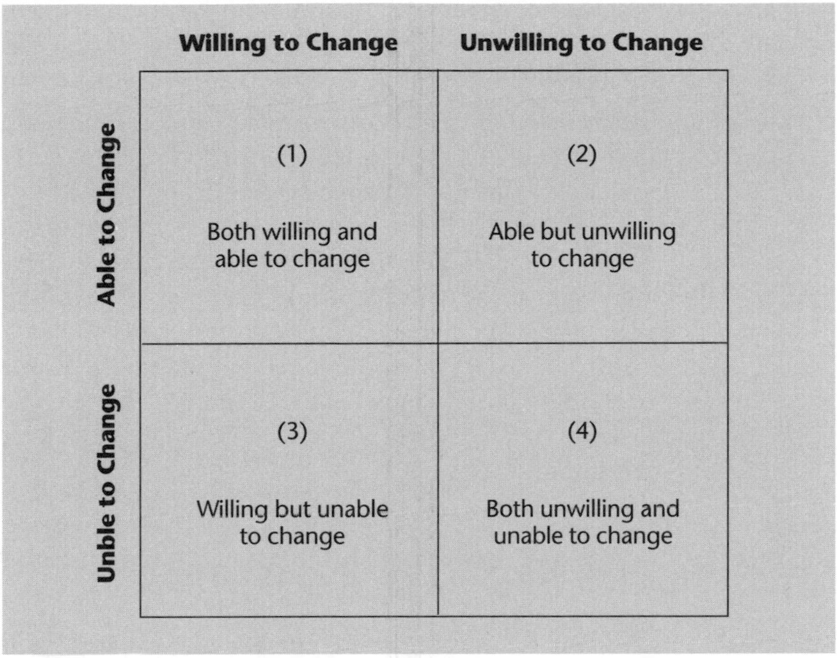

	Willing to Change	**Unwilling to Change**
Able to Change	(1) Both willing and able to change	(2) Able but unwilling to change
Unble to Change	(3) Willing but unable to change	(4) Both unwilling and unable to change

Figure 7   Relationship Between Willingness and Ability to Change

effectiveness of supervision, feedback, cooperation, encouragement, support, and the information one receives.

Lack of ability may appear to be resistance, but inability and unwillingness are actually quite different. As Figure 7 indicates, if we take into consideration both willingness and ability to change, we can distinguish four scenarios. These can be described as follows:

Scenario 1: Both willing and able to change. In this scenario, the person both wants to change and can change. This combination of factors is the one most clearly associated with readiness to change.

Scenario 2: Able but unwilling to change. In this scenario, the person can change but doesn't want to. This combination of factors is the one most clearly associated with resistance to change.

Scenario 3: Willing but unable to change. In this scenario, the person wants to change but can't. In other words, the person lacks the knowledge, skills, confidence, and/or resources necessary to change. Under this set of conditions, it's important to find out specifically why the person can't change or doesn't believe he/she can change, so that appropriate corrective measures can be taken.

Scenario 4: Both unwilling and unable to change. In this scenario, the person neither wants to change nor can change. This set of conditions poses an interesting challenge diagnostically. Specifically, it's important to determine if the person is really unwilling *and* unable to change. Sometimes people say they can't change when they really don't want to change. When this happens they would still resist change, even if you helped them gain the necessary knowledge, skills, confidence, and/or resources. In other cases, people might want to change if they were able to. Helping them gain the necessary knowledge, skills, confidence, and/or resources, therefore, could produce readiness to change.

Positive and Negative Resistance

I don't want to give the impression that change is always positive or that resistance is always negative. It's crucial to bear in mind that any change, large or small, will make people different from what they were before. There's no such thing as a change with a neutral impact: people will either be better or worse off because of it. Those of us who are proponents of change should never forget this.

By itself, change is inherently neither good nor bad. Although change can be evaluated by its consequences, it's impossible to know in advance if a change will turn out to be positive or negative. After taking all the relevant factors into consideration, there are times when it's best not to make a change. For example, let's say that you have an assistant, Bill Arnold, who is not as efficient in his position as some other employee on your staff would be. Bill's rapport with those under his supervision, however, is so strong that replacing him could have a very disruptive effect on the other employees. In this case, you determine that the costs of the proposed change outweigh the benefits and therefore decide not to replace Bill.

It is also necessary to recognize that every organization requires a certain amount of stability to function effectively. Constant change would lead to chaos. Organizations also need employees who want to continue doing what they are already good at. If managers spend too much time preparing employees for advancement, which is a type of change, no one will be available to do work that needs to be done now, which could jeopardize the organization. A major challenge of any manager is locating the balance between change and stability. Finding this position decreases the probability that a manager will inadvertently encourage change that ends up harming the organization.

Not only are there times when change is inadvisable, but there are also times when resistance is the best action. Unfortunately, the word *resistance* often has a negative connotation, but at times it is the most effective response. During World War II, for example, *resistance* was a positive term. Consider also that a healthy body resists infection, and this kind of resistance is not only adaptable but essential for the preservation of life.

If people's beliefs, values, and behaviors provide them with constructive ways of meeting needs, then it's adaptive and healthy to hold on to them and to resist change. Viable beliefs and values and effective behaviors bring continuity to one's life, which is necessary to meet needs in an orderly manner. Some changes disrupt this process and cause people to become disorganized and less productive. In these situations resisting change is in a person's best interests to resist change.

Thus, there are times when resistance is a problem and times when it's a solution. We can distinguish four possibilities. First, if people are willing to make positive or necessary changes, resistance is not an issue. The key is to gather enough information to determine that the changes actually are positive or necessary. Second, if people resist positive or necessary changes, resistance is a problem. An example is refusing to get the required training for career advancement. Third, if people resist negative or unnecessary changes, resistance is a solution. An example is trying to block a decision that has good short-term but bad long-range consequences. Finally, if people are willing to make negative or unnecessary changes, lack of resistance could be a problem. Some examples are changing a product without conducting a market analysis, speculating with money one can't afford to lose, or hiring someone without checking references. In situations like these, people should actually be encouraged to resist change.

Your Resistance Is Showing

Let me make a bold statement: You have no business trying to overcome resistance in someone else, or even complaining about it, if you are unwilling to change. As someone involved in leading others through change, you must be a role model that others can emulate in situations in which change would be constructive. Before you can function effectively as such a role model, you need to ask yourself some difficult but challenging questions, and you must be honest enough to admit it when your answers are less than completely favorable:

▲ Do you have facts, beliefs, or values that inhibit your ability to change? If so, what are they?
▲ Have you examined the implications of your facts, beliefs, and values for yourself and others?
▲ Which of your beliefs might be non-empirically based?
▲ What evidence do you have to substantiate your facts and beliefs?
▲ Are you willing to scrutinize your facts, beliefs, and values regularly to see what part they play in either promoting or interfering with your willingness to change?
▲ If you recognize a value or belief that restricts positive change, are you willing to change it?
▲ If someone confronts you with evidence contrary to your facts or beliefs, are you willing to consider that evidence without becoming defensive?

None of us can claim a perfect score in our responses to these questions. Expecting this of ourselves would deny our humanity. But, whereas some people never grapple with these questions; you cannot afford this luxury. Since your decisions affect the lives of others, you must have a thorough awareness of your facts, beliefs, and values as you make those decisions. No one can force you to engage in this kind of introspection; it has to be something you do voluntarily. My aim is to convince you that scrutinizing your facts, beliefs, and values is necessary for effective leadership, so that you will want to do this.

For several other reasons, it is important to notice any factors that might interfere with your willingness to change. To begin with, your actions are visible to others in the organization. You will be expected to be a clear thinker, capable of logically evaluating a situation by considering all relevant variables, then arriving at the most rational conclusion. Much of your credibility hinges on how adequately you do this. People who do not appear to think logically are labeled "irrational," "impulsive," "stubborn," "bullheaded," and "egotistical." Needless to say, if others believe you are what any of these words imply, they may not have confidence in you.

In addition, if others view you as someone not open to alternative views, they might not bother to share ideas with you. This will prevent you from receiving information you need to make the best possible decisions. By remaining open to others' ideas and being willing to modify your own views, you will be creating a climate conducive to positive change.

You also need to keep in mind that your actions could actually be the source of resistance among others. If you stubbornly hold on to your own beliefs and insist that your way is right in spite of others' opinions, you increase the likelihood that your way will be resisted. There are times, of course, when you will need to make decisions that others don't like, and it is quite possible that you cannot make a decision with which everyone agrees. This is one of the hard facts of life. Nevertheless, if others see you as being open to their views and willing to objectively hear them out when a difference of opinion exists, they will be more likely to support you even if your decision is not what they want.

It is crucial that others see you are being fair; it can be devastating to be seen as arbitrary, capricious, or insensitive to the views, needs, and desires of others. Others are capable of believing that you are all these bad things, even if you're not. To reduce the possibility that others will develop mistaken beliefs about you, you must give them regular evidence that you are both unbiased and open to the ideas of others.

A final consideration, perhaps the most crucial, is that the actions you take based on your beliefs and values affect other people's lives for better or worse. Carrying this responsibility requires you to guard against the possibility that your beliefs could be mistaken or that your values could lead others astray.

For example, if you believe that Joe Cardwell is incapable of learning enough to succeed at more demanding jobs, you may decide that you shouldn't waste time helping Joe improve. It could be, however, that Joe is capable of learning, but you are unable to teach him what he needs to know. Your belief provides you with an excuse not to spend much time with Joe, while it deprives him of the opportunity to advance within the organization. Just because you've tried everything you know to help someone like Joe doesn't mean that you've exhausted the alternatives. There may be methods you're not aware of, your teaching style might clash with his learning style, or you might not be the best one to work with Joe. In this case, it would be imperative to examine your beliefs and the actions that result from them. If you resist doing this and insist that you're right, you may deprive someone of a chance to become a more effective and capable person.

Identifying Resistance in Others

Symptoms, the specific behaviors people use to resist change, fall into two categories, *active* and *passive* resistance. Following are some examples of both types.

Active resistance

Being critical	Blaming/Accusing	Blocking
Finding fault	Sabotaging	Undermining
Ridiculing	Intimidating/Threatening	Starting rumors
Appealing to fear	Manipulating	Arguing
Using facts selectively	Distorting facts	

Passive resistance

Agreeing verbally but not following through

Failing to implement change

Procrastinating/dragging feet

Feigning ignorance

Withholding information, suggestions, help, or support

Standing by and allowing the change to fail

These behaviors tell us that people are resisting change but they don't tell us why. To find the causes, we must understand a person's facts, beliefs, and values. Since we can't literally see these, the role they play in creating resistance can be difficult to isolate—difficult, but not impossible. Accurately identifying these variables will never be an exact science, but we must do the best we can, in spite of limitations.

Fortunately, we have a powerful source of information to help us with this task: observation of what people do and say. Everything someone does or says is a clue that can provide insight into the causes of resistance. Such information has always been available, but it is seldom utilized fully. Consequently, attempts to deal with resistance are often unsystematic and ineffective.

It is risky to try to assess the causes of resistance by observing only what a person does. People misinterpret others' behavior all the time.

Watching people in action supplies clues, but additional information from what they say is almost always necessary to reach an accurate diagnosis.

The Difficulty of Inferring Beliefs from Actions

Observe both what people do and what they say in trying to discover what they really believe because

Any specific act can represent multiple possible beliefs.

People can act the same even though the beliefs behind their behavior are very different.

People can base their actions on mistaken beliefs not readily apparent to you or them.

In addition, people are capable of acting inconsistently with their beliefs. Some people, for example, might sign a petition asking for higher wages not because they believe they deserve more money but because of peer pressure. If you saw these people signing the petition and assumed it was because they believed they were underpaid, you would be making an error. In this case, you could learn much more by talking to the people than by only observing what they do.

The key is to determine whether beliefs are based on accurate or inaccurate interpretations of experience. Of course, resistance can and frequently does stem from beliefs based on solid empirical evidence. Resistance of this kind is usually much more difficult to overcome than resistance that can be traced to mistaken or inaccurate interpretations, because people are resisting with "good reason." You must be aware of the basis upon which beliefs are held so that you can deal effectively with resistance when it surfaces.

The Difficulty of Inferring Values from Actions

Everything someone does reflects one or more values, because values represent convictions about desirable pursuits. This doesn't necessarily mean, however, that the values are obvious. Sometimes people engage in undesirable activity in order to pursue one of their values. For example, a man may be cleaning up trash at the end of a workday, even though he isn't required to do so. On the surface it may appear that he values cleanliness. If we examine the reasons for this behavior, we may find that he greatly dislikes cleaning but does it because he believes it will help him keep his job. Therefore, job security, not cleanliness, is the value motivating his behavior. We would not discover this by merely observing what he does. Talking to him, however, could reveal his values.

We can also tell a lot about people's values by observing what they don't do. Before we conclude that they lack certain values, however, we must rule out other factors. I have already discussed the inhibiting role played by fear in the choices people make. A person may want to do something but decide not to, because of fear. Sometimes people act because they're afraid not to. Thus, security is the value motivating behavior, although it may appear that some other value guides them. People are motivated to stay clear of perceived danger as well as to pursue what they desire, and when fear is intense, protecting oneself from perceived danger pushes other values into the background.

People's beliefs often play a prominent, if disguised, role in this process. Often mistaken beliefs generate fear, causing people to pursue security as a value. Thus, additional data revealing the actual purposes served by a person's actions can be crucial.

Don't Jump to Conclusions

In your efforts to locate the causes of resistance, base your inferences on evidence you can clearly substantiate. You are on solid ground if you say to yourself, "Her statement suggests that she disagrees with my decision," without giving in to the temptation to add, "therefore she must have something against me." Avoid drawing conclusions or making generalizations that go beyond what you can see and hear. It's all right to formulate hypotheses, but it's to your advantage to collect as much evidence as possible before inferring the cause of resistance and deciding on action.

Most important, keep an open mind. This will allow you to consider additional evidence, especially if it contradicts previous inferences. You can't afford to develop a vested interest in your own conclusions. An unwillingness to objectively consider additional evidence is a sign of resistance on *your* part, which will get in the way of your ability to solve a problem. Remain humble. Don't tell yourself you need to be right; dealing with resistance is hard enough without getting in your own way.

Build a Catalog of Facts, Beliefs, and Values Held by Others

Identifying others' facts, beliefs, and values is an ongoing process, not a single event that occurs when resistance is encountered. As you work with people over an extended period of time, you will have many opportunities to observe them in a wide variety of situations. You will be able to see what they say and do under routine conditions and during times of change. Through this process, you can develop a catalog of their facts, beliefs, and values. Investing the time and effort to do this will pay off when you plan a change that will affect others. Your inventory will help you anticipate resistance and take steps to prevent or minimize it.

In addition, the information in your catalog can be an invaluable resource whenever resistance surfaces. Without the catalog, you may be unable to understand why people are resisting change. With it, you can put that resistance into perspective by relating it to facts, beliefs, and values. When observing what someone does, ask yourself, "What fact, belief, or value is being reflected by what this person is doing?" Similarly, when listening to someone, ask yourself, "What fact, belief, or value is being conveyed by what this person is saying?" By consistently asking yourself these questions, and putting the data together, not only will you come to understand people more fully, but you will be able to more effectively locate the causes of resistance when it occurs. In the next chapter I discuss the resistance matrix, which will assist you in building a catalog of people's facts, beliefs, and values.

Current and Desired Organizational Beliefs, Values, and Behaviors

Purpose

This exercise is designed to help clarify both current organizational beliefs, values, and behaviors, and those that are desired in the future. The exercise takes about one hour.

Procedure for Group Use

1. Explain that before initiating organizational change, it's important to know where you are now and where you'd like to go.

2. Divide participants into groups of four to six.

3. Hand out a copy of the worksheets to each participant, and give these instructions:

   I'd like one group to list on a flip chart the current beliefs, values, and behaviors of people in the organization, and the other group to list the beliefs, values, and behaviors they'd like to see in the future.

   (Note: If you have more than two groups, assign half of the groups to work on the "current" and the other half to work on the "desired.")

4. Give the groups fifteen minutes to complete their lists.

5. Ask each group to share their results with the whole group, starting with the "current" group(s).

6. Discuss the results with the whole group:

   What differences do you see?

   What needs to happen to get from the "current" to the "desired"?

   What obstacles could get in the way of the desired changes?

7. Ask for and respond to questions.

   (Note: Keep the flip charts generated by the groups, if you plan to have these participants do Exercise 6 in Chapter 10, Plan of Action for Overcoming Resistance to Change.)

Procedure for Individual Use

1. On the next two pages, write down the current beliefs, values, and behaviors of people in your organization, and the beliefs, values, and behaviors you desire in the future.

2. You will refer back to this information when you complete the Change Planning Guide at the end of Chapter 10.

Current

Beliefs

Values

Behaviors

Desired

Beliefs

Values

Behaviors

7

Locating Causes
of Resistance

In everyday conversation, people often use the term *resistance* to indicate that others are against certain ways of thinking or behaving. Some expressions are limited to specifying whether resistance is present or absent. Thus we hear statements such as, "There is resistance to implementing the new procedures," "Some people will resist that idea," or "Similar ideas have been resisted in the past." While such statements are common, they are not very informative. They tell us nothing about why there is resistance or what to do about it. Furthermore, they misrepresent the complex nature of resistance.

Others go one step further and express the degree to which resistance is either present or absent. We hear, for example, "There is a great deal of resistance among certain employees" or "His resistance isn't as great as it was last week." The intensity of resistance can be thought of as existing on a continuum extending from none at one end to extreme at the other end. To specify the intensity of resistance in a particular instance, we can rely only upon a subjective estimate. As a result, people frequently disagree on just how much resistance is present. People need to discuss their estimates so that such disagreements can be identified and resolved and appropriate actions taken.

Although the *intensity* of resistance is an important consideration, it is only one of three relevant variables that must be taken into account to fully describe and explain resistance in a specific situation. The other two variables are the *sources* and *focuses* of resistance. Resistance can stem from five major sources (facts, descriptive beliefs, evaluative

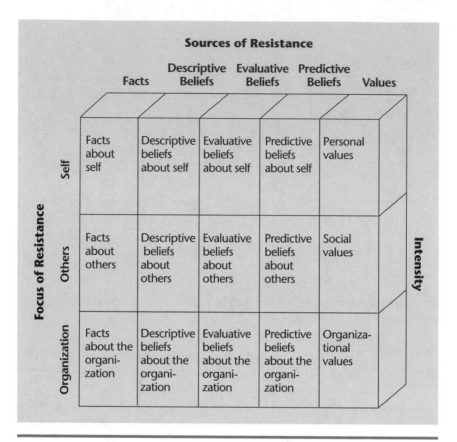

Sources of Resistance

	Facts	Descriptive Beliefs	Evaluative Beliefs	Predictive Beliefs	Values
Self	Facts about self	Descriptive beliefs about self	Evaluative beliefs about self	Predictive beliefs about self	Personal values
Others	Facts about others	Descriptive beliefs about others	Evaluative beliefs about others	Predictive beliefs about others	Social values
Organization	Facts about the organization	Descriptive beliefs about the organization	Evaluative beliefs about the organization	Predictive beliefs about the organization	Organizational values

Focus of Resistance

Intensity

Figure 8   Resistance Matrix

beliefs, predictive beliefs, and values) and can focus on self, other people, or the organization. Taken together, these variables form a three-dimensional resistance matrix, which is depicted in Figure 8.

The resistance matrix permits us to make meaningful statements about the causes of resistance. We can say, for example, that an employee demonstrates a small amount of resistance stemming from a descriptive belief regarding other people (i.e., they are out to get him), and that another employee shows considerable resistance to technology because of a certain social value (i.e., he wants to communicate with others in person, instead of through e-mail). Such statements give us a broader understanding of resistance, revealing its full complexity.

Using the resistance matrix, let's look at some things people say that can help you identify whether resistance is stemming from facts, descriptive beliefs, evaluative beliefs, predictive beliefs, or values. This information can then be added to observations of what they do to help you diagnose the reasons for resistance. Once you have gathered all relevant information regarding the intensity, source, and focus of resistance, you should be able to develop an effective strategy for dealing with the resistance.

Facts

Two issues are especially relevant in trying to determine the role played by facts in particular instances of resistance. First, you need to find out if you are actually dealing with facts, and second, you need to see how facts are used to foster resistance. In the first instance, absolute proof is needed for something to qualify as a fact. Anything short of this makes it a belief. So, the issue of evidence is key here. People often fail to distinguish between facts and beliefs in their mind and in the way they talk. Thus, people confuse facts with beliefs when they say "I know . . .," I'm convinced that . . .," or "I'm absolutely sure that . . ." Watch carefully for beliefs presented as facts; if a statement can't be backed up by definitive evidence, then it is a belief. It is especially important for you to make these distinctions because many people want their beliefs to sound like facts in order to be convincing.

The second question—how facts are used—is trickier. When people resist change, they may selectively bring up facts that support their case. In other words, they may present some but not all of the facts. Sometimes this is deliberate, and sometimes it is unintentional. In either case, you must listen closely when people present facts and try to identify other relevant information. Otherwise, your ability to see how selective use of facts is fostering resistance will be greatly limited.

For example, a woman may not apply for a promotion because on two previous occasions she was turned down for advancement. The woman has received improved performance reviews lately and scored high on a number of qualifying examinations for various positions. When she explains why she didn't apply for the promotion, she may present the former facts but not the latter. You, of course, need to know as much as possible about her situation to understand why she is using facts selectively to resist change.

Facts are useful to people who want to escape or avoid something they are afraid of, because facts make such convincing rationalizations.

One of the best ways for people to get you off their backs is to bring up irrefutable evidence ("I always got low grades in math, so you should get someone else to teach these methods for measuring quality"). This puts you in the position of having to deal with their evidence on their terms. Unfortunately, they can be so convincing that they end up preventing themselves from doing something that would enhance their career.

Facts, of course, are highly relevant and necessary when people are trying to identify the causes of a problem, make a decision, or consider a proposed change. You may be presenting facts in favor of your view, while others may be using facts to argue for their perspective. The problem is that facts can be used either to shed light on a situation or to distort what's being discussed. If the discussion is conducted in a manner conducive to objective and rational consideration of all relevant facts, this can be a productive process.

When the level of resistance is intense, however, the ability of people to logically present and consider facts is reduced. If people are determined to have their own way, emotional and ego involvement in their views will interfere with their ability to present all facts and their willingness to listen to your facts. Intense emotion and reason don't mix. In an atmosphere charged with strong feelings, your ability to use logical persuasion to lower resistance will be reduced. Change through consensus building requires a situation in which people cooperate and don't feel threatened. Threat leads to defensiveness and conflict, increasing the possibility that facts will be used to serve self-interests rather than mutual interests.

On some occasions it may be difficult to understand why a fact is mentioned at all. In these situations, your best bet is to look at the fact within the context of what's being discussed. If people are trying to influence you, they will probably pick the most opportune time to state a revealing fact; that is, they will select the time within the discussion when presenting the fact will most benefit their case. Although you may detect the possibility that the fact is being used to resist change, it is wise to check the accuracy of your inference by gathering further information. Once someone states a fact, she is in essence, showing her hand. You can follow up by asking, "Based on that fact, what do you think should be done?" This will allow you to avoid making an incorrect assumption about why the fact is being presented.

For example, facts about the organization are often presented at just the right time to undermine a proposed change. In other words, they are not brought out for added perspective, but to persuade you not to make the change you have in mind. Also, some facts about the organization may be selectively presented, while others are either ignored or minimized ("Wc tried the same thing two years ago"). If people disagree with your proposal, frequently they develop their case against the change before discussing it with you; therefore, your ability to anticipate these arguments in advance will be crucial to lowering resistance. The worst position you can be in is to be caught off guard by someone else's facts. Responding off the top of your head could lower your chances of handling the situation effectively. Do your homework! Following are a few typical statements of "facts" used to resist change. Use your own experience to add to the list.

Facts About Self

"My doctor told me I shouldn't subject myself to too much stress."

"All my friends are in this department."

"I've been in this job for thirty years."

"I never had a course in accounting."

"I've never written a proposal before."

"I failed math in high school."

"That isn't in my job description."

"I don't like change."

Facts About Others

"They just filed for bankruptcy."

"He was fired from his last job."

"Joe doesn't even have a college degree. Why should he get the promotion?"

"I understand she has three children."

"Other companies that buy supplies from them say they never deliver on time."

"He's black, you know."

"I hope you're aware that she's a leader in the local women's caucus."

"He doesn't have any sales experience."

"You said you weren't going to make any major changes this year."

Facts About the Organization

"We pay skilled workers less than any other electronics firm in town."

"The turnover rate is already 25 percent higher this year."

"The last time we tried that we were slapped with a five thousand dollar fine."

"Keep in mind that grievances have been increasing during the past six months."

"Our office already has more people in it than any other. How can you expect us to work effectively if you move more employees in here?"

"We haven't received the training we were promised."

"Why should we do that? We haven't received a salary increase in three years."

The relationship between facts and beliefs is very complex. Sometimes facts are the major cause of resistance, and if they can be identified and placed in perspective, associated beliefs may also change. At other times, beliefs are the major cause of resistance, and identifying and dealing with seemingly relevant facts will have no effect upon the beliefs. Even if people can produce facts as a way of arguing against change ("We only have $50,000 in the budget"), however, they will always have beliefs about those facts. Upon questioning, therefore, people might respond, "$50,000 isn't enough money," which is a belief that goes beyond the facts. Whether or not there's enough money is most likely a matter of opinion. When you first spot signs of resistance, it's sometimes difficult to tell if the primary cause is facts, beliefs, or a combination. Only when you begin to piece together many bits of information will the relationship between these variables become clearer.

Descriptive Beliefs

Recall that *descriptive beliefs* are not facts but subjective interpretations that define for someone what is true and false. People rely on descriptive beliefs to interpret the past ("Hiring him was a mistake") and the present ("It takes us too much time to make decisions"). Descriptive beliefs have to do with what things mean. For example, in the statement, "We didn't get the contract, so we'll probably have to let some people go," the first part is a fact, and the second part is a descriptive belief that gives a meaning to the fact.

The Misunderstanding

Nat Reed was manager of an engineering department that develops modular electronic components. In this particular company, engineers working in teams had proven to be most productive. Of ten teams, all but one, Bill Riley and Mike Crane, were on schedule with project deadlines. Since Bill and Mike frequently argued, they were behind schedule and jeopardized a large project's success. When Nat talked with them jointly, they began a shouting match, blaming each other for delays. Not sure how he should handle this, the manager simply told them to speed it up or he would be forced to consider more serious action.

Despite this, Bill and Mike's problem grew worse. Nat considered reassigning them to other teams, but all the other engineers worked well together. Since a heavy production schedule would not allow time to train new engineers, he was reluctant to fire them. Therefore, the only viable alternative was to get at the root of the problem and attempt to resolve it.

Nat searched for clues to how the conflict began. He talked to other engineers in the department—the problem was well known to everyone—and to Bill and Mike separately. Through this process, he found that the conflict began before the two were assigned to work together. Someone told Bill that Mike drove off his last partner because he preferred to work alone. Bill feared that Mike would also try to get rid of him (descriptive belief) and was defensive around Mike from the beginning. Someone also told Mike that Bill was assigned to work with him even though he wanted to work with someone else. So he believed that Bill did not want to work with him (descriptive belief), which made him defensive also.

The resistance that prevented the two engineers from accepting their team assignment stemmed from descriptive beliefs they had about each other that were never checked for accuracy. Nat learned when talking with Mike that his last partner left because he was unhappy about his salary and opportunities for advancement. He also found out that Mike preferred working with a partner. In a separate talk with Bill, Nat discovered that he preferred working with a close friend but did not object to working with Mike until he was told that Mike drove off his last partner. Nat brought the two together to help clarify misunderstandings. Both were surprised and relieved to find that initial beliefs about each other were unfounded. After this clarification, they began to work harmoniously and their production increased.

Whether people establish correct or incorrect descriptive beliefs (meanings) depends largely on what they regard as evidence. As we've discussed in previous chapters, fewer errors are made when people rely on empirical evidence to test the validity of their beliefs. Empirical evidence is usually more effective than simply taking someone's word for it ("If you say so, then it must be true") or blindly assuming you are correct ("I can't prove it, but I know I'm right," or "Trust me on this one").

Of course, the empirical data necessary to validate or invalidate descriptive beliefs is more tangible and easier to gather in some situations than in others. For example, you can validate your belief that a particular employee is reliable by checking previous attendance records. On the other hand, your belief that participative management is an effective way to make decisions may take months or years to validate. Nevertheless, it is possible to monitor behavioral changes over time and use the evidence to assess the viability of your belief. The key is finding appropriate yardsticks against which to gauge relevant beliefs for any given situation.

Descriptive beliefs form the basis for three types of fallacies that often result in resistance to change: the deductive fallacy, the inductive fallacy, and the cause-effect fallacy. Let me describe how each of these fallacies works.

The *deductive fallacy* occurs when someone starts with a general belief or premise and incorrectly concludes that, since this belief is true, other specific beliefs must also be true. Sometimes the starting premise is wrong; at other times it is accurate but the beliefs deduced from it are mistaken. A manager may, for example, believe that employees are motivated only by self-interest and deduce from this that they can't be trusted, that they won't do anything unless there's something in it for them, that they'll cheat the organization if they have an opportunity, and that they will take advantage of others to get ahead. As a result of these beliefs, the manager will watch employees like a hawk, relating to them more as prisoners than co-workers.

If You're a Manager, You're Against Me

Kent Smithson was a new assembly-line worker whose manager was Hal Kaubmaun. Where Kent had worked, he was an active union member and had bitter arguments with management over wages and working conditions. He had been fired for this conduct. Because of this experience, Kent believed that management was against labor in any company (descriptive belief) and would do little to meet their needs (predictive belief). He also believed that labor had to fight for any improvements in working conditions (descriptive belief). Since this had been true in the past, he concluded that it would be true under Hal's management (deductive fallacy).

Hal noticed that Kent was somewhat hostile toward him from the beginning. This didn't become an issue until Hal established a committee to recommend improvements in labor-management relations. Kent opposed the concept of the committee and led a group that tried to convince laborers that this committee was an attempt by management to placate employees without really dealing with the issues. Hal felt that Kent misunderstood his motivation and decided to talk with him. Unfortunately, the meeting went badly. Kent was so convinced he was right that he wouldn't listen to Hal.

Because of this, Hal decided that he needed to form another strategy to deal with growing resistance toward the committee. Hal realized that Kent couldn't be talked out of his beliefs, and the only viable solution would be for the committee to provide concrete, tangible results. Therefore, he ignored Kent's opposing group and worked on accomplishing definite goals through the committee. After a few months, it became increasingly clear that Hal was genuinely interested in improving working conditions, drawing upon employees' input. As major reforms were instituted, resistance toward the committee dwindled rapidly. Soon, only Kent opposed the committee, and even he softened. It was difficult for Kent to maintain his beliefs while facing the reality of Hal's actions. Kent, though still skeptical about managers, no longer functioned as a rebel without a cause.

An *inductive fallacy* takes place when someone starts with one or more specific beliefs and incorrectly concludes that, since these beliefs are true, a general premise must also be true. Again, the specific beliefs could be mistaken, and even if they are accurate, the general conclusion for which they serve as evidence could be false. For example, Sara

Clemens, new manager of the sales division, might believe that male employees are deliberately trying to keep contact with her as brief and formal as possible, that they share information with her only when it's absolutely necessary, and that they are whispering about her behind her back. From these specific beliefs, she may draw the general conclusion that the male employees resent her because she got the management position. It's possible that Sara will simply accept this conclusion without checking into the specific beliefs leading to it. This may inhibit her ability to relate to the male employees, making her beliefs a self-fulfilling prophesy. If she seeks additional evidence to validate or invalidate the specific beliefs, on the other hand, she may find that not only are the specific beliefs wrong, but the general conclusion is mistaken. Even if the initial beliefs are corroborated, she can use the additional evidence to help initiate a plan to deal with the problem.

The *cause-effect fallacy* occurs when someone mistakenly concludes that since two beliefs are true, one belief causes the other. One or both beliefs could be wrong, but even if they are correct, it could be incorrect to assume that one belief causes the other. To illustrate, during a staff meeting last week Tom Childs believed be was being more assertive than usual. Today he received a performance evaluation that was lower than he believed he deserved. Tom concluded that his assertive behavior caused his manager to give him a lower evaluation. Since the manager completed the report before the staff meeting, Tom was mistaken. Unfortunately, Tom didn't try to find out if his belief was correct. Strongly convinced that he was right, he decided not to discuss the issue with the manager and filed a grievance with the union instead. Needless to say, this mistaken conclusion caused unnecessary difficulty for Tom, the manager, the union, and other workers in the unit.

The deductive, inductive, and cause-effect fallacies demonstrate how descriptive beliefs can lead people to jump to conclusions. Of course, the ability to formulate conclusions is an important part of the thinking process. Conclusions can help people make decisions and exercise judgment in very complex situations. Nevertheless, conclusions are only as good as the specific facts and beliefs upon which they are based. People must strive to reach sound conclusions based upon the most solid evidence available and be willing to consider new evidence whenever necessary. On the other hand, jumping to conclusions based on mistaken beliefs and inadequate evidence puts people in the position of spending most of their time struggling with their own illusive beliefs—like a boxer fighting his shadow.

Descriptive beliefs can focus on self, others, or the organization. Descriptive beliefs about self often play a key role in people's openness to change. This is particularly true of beliefs about what one can and can't do. For example, if someone states a fact such as "I've never tried that before," we still don't know if the person will resist change. Following up this statement with "I'm a slow learner" is likely to evoke fear leading to escape or avoidance behavior; whereas following it up with "Effort is the key" is more likely to produce confidence resulting in proactive, goal-directed behavior. A lot of what either happens or doesn't happen in people's careers depends upon whether the beliefs they hold about their abilities are viable or unviable.

The Vindictive Employee

Charles Kelly was a skilled machine operator in a metal products company. His manager was John Luboff. One day John mentioned his displeasure about the quality of work Charles accepted from apprentice machine operators he supervised. Charles became defensive, arguing that the work standards were unrealistically high for people with little experience. John was surprised by Charles's defensive response but decided to forget the incident.

Several months later Charles and several machinists applied for an opening as foreman. When someone else got the position, Charles became furious. He believed that John had given him a bad reference because of their discussion about work quality (cause-effect fallacy). He became belligerent and bad-mouthed John to other employees. When John heard this, his first impulse was to fire Charles. To John such behavior was inexcusable. Fortunately, however, John didn't act on his anger and tried to find a rational explanation for Charles's behavior.

John decided to discuss it with Charles. Although Charles was reluctant, he revealed his belief about John. John was surprised, because he considered the incident minor and had fully supported Charles for foreman. When John showed Charles a very favorable reference letter, Charles realized that he was wrong and apologized. Both agreed to avoid future situations like this by more open communication.

Descriptive beliefs about others can also be used to resist change. The most damaging beliefs in this category are those in which people impute motives to others. Some examples are "He's just out for himself," "She likes to make others look bad," "He's probably trying to add her to his list of conquests," or "She just pretends to be supportive of the project." In my experience, guessing at people's motives is prevalent in most organizations. Since beliefs of this kind usually take the form of gossip, those being whispered about don't have a chance to defend themselves. Behavior of this sort has a devastating effect on interpersonal relationships. Those hearing the gossip are tainted by it and, even if they don't agree with it, seeds of doubt have been planted. Also, they're left to wonder if others are gossiping about them. Unless people have the courage to bring their beliefs about each other out in the open and deal with them directly, a climate of acceptance, mutual respect, and trust never materializes.

Other beliefs take the form of critical descriptions of people's weaknesses or limitations. Examples are "He just doesn't have what it takes to do the job," and "She never follows through on her commitments." When beliefs like these are stated, probe for information that will allow you to accurately pinpoint the reason for resistance. Asking such questions as "Could you tell me more about why you feel the way you do?" can help you do this.

In addition, negative descriptive beliefs about the organization are frequently responsible for resistance to change. These beliefs are reflected in such statements as "This company doesn't care about its employees," "We're treated like numbers, not persons," or "It's impossible to get ahead around here." Since they can easily lead to anger, frustration, and other contagious emotions, it's important to give people opportunities where such beliefs can be aired objectively. There's no substitute for being viewed as someone willing to listen and to give opinions an impartial hearing. If people don't come to you to discuss their beliefs about a situation, it will be difficult to identify the reasons for resistance. Of course, being regarded as someone who is fair develops over time. In fact, not doing this is often a major cause of resistance in organizations.

Following is another list of typical statements designed to aid you in locating descriptive beliefs responsible for resistance.

Descriptive Beliefs About Self

"I don't think I could accept that change."

"I'm too busy to do this."

"I'm too shy to work in a large group."

"I don't have the energy for that much responsibility."

"I'm a follower, not a leader."

"A man has got to know his limitations."

"I don't have anything to contribute to a team."

"The pressure's too much for me."

"Yes, but . . ."

Descriptive Beliefs About Others

"He just tells people what they want to hear."

"I don't think moving her to another department would solve the problem."

"I wouldn't discuss this with him, because he can't keep anything to himself."

"He pretends to be busy to avoid additional work."

"He makes those changes just to harass us."

"She never seems to understand our point of view."

"He always passes the buck to someone else."

"He's more concerned with protecting his security than anything else."

"Watch out for him."

Descriptive Beliefs About the Organization

"We're underpaid for what we're asked to do."

"The fringe benefits offered by this company are really low."

"In this company, it's not what you know, it's who you know that counts."

"This organization is all form and no substance."

"We're evaluated too frequently."

"This company isn't open to new ideas."

"Opportunities for promotion around here only go to those who don't make waves."

"This organization is more rigid than the one I came from."

"That's just the way we do things around here."

Evaluative Beliefs

While descriptive beliefs are interpretations about what's true or false, *evaluative beliefs* define what's good or bad. Descriptive beliefs assign meaning to experience, both past and present, but evaluative beliefs go beyond this and judge the meanings assigned. Perhaps comparing a descriptive belief with an evaluative belief will help clarify this distinction. Consider the statement "A thorough knowledge of continuous quality improvement is necessary to manage effectively today." This descriptive belief asserts that a relationship exists between knowledge of CQI and effective management. Now consider the statement "Continuous quality improvement is good for an organization." It's important to understand evaluative beliefs, because if we are proposing a change that others believe is "good," chances are they will support it. If they believe the proposed change is "bad," however, the probability is increased that they will resist it. Hence, we need to be concerned with people's definitions of "good" and "bad" as they apply to specific situations.

It's very difficult to validate or invalidate evaluative beliefs, because by definition they are subjective judgments. Nevertheless, there are a few methods available to assist this process. To begin with, evaluative beliefs often stem from facts and descriptive beliefs that may be accurate or inaccurate. Inaccurate facts and unviable descriptive beliefs will have a more negative impact on evaluative beliefs than accurate facts and viable descriptive beliefs. For example, take the statement "Jim just laid off Bill. He could have laid off someone else. I think that's terrible!" The first sentence is a fact, the second one is a descriptive belief, and the third one is an evaluative belief. While the fact is accurate, it's possible that the descriptive belief is inaccurate. In this case, the evaluative belief is based on the assumption that the descriptive belief is true. If it turns out that Bill is the only one who could have been laid off, however, then the evaluative belief is out of line. Checking the accuracy of related facts and descriptive beliefs can help counter evaluative beliefs based on faulty conclusions.

When people offer a descriptive belief, there's almost always one or more evaluative beliefs linked to it. These evaluative beliefs may or may not be stated. Assume, for instance, that someone states this descriptive belief: "He always gives other people the assignments he doesn't like." If we ask, "How do you feel about that?" a few people might say, "I'm not sure how I feel," but many more would go on to reveal, "I think it's very irresponsible." Questions of this kind are useful in bringing implied evaluative beliefs out into the open. The additional information might reveal the cause of a person's resistance.

Another way of scrutinizing evaluative beliefs is more subjective. It can be phrased, "Does the belief help or hinder people's efforts to meet their needs?" My view is that evaluative beliefs that inhibit need-fulfilling behavior are excess baggage that ought to be discarded. What difference does it make if you can produce evidence to support a certain judgment, if the result is that your needs remain unmet? It's important, therefore, to assess the consequences of holding various evaluative beliefs by asking, "What affect does this belief have on my life and on the lives of those with whom I come into contact?" If we routinely took stock of our evaluative beliefs, we would have a better basis not only for determining if the interpretations behind them are true, but also for deciding if the beliefs are worth having.

Now let's examine evaluative beliefs as they pertain to self, others, and the organization. Whether people like themselves and the quality of their work are key factors in determining if they will resist change. Consider the statements "I guess my low score on the test proves again how stupid I am" and "I knew I would fail; I must really be incompetent." It is rare for people to actually say these things to someone else, but it is quite common for them to form private negative judgments about themselves. Let's examine these two statements.

In the first statement a fact (low test score) is used as evidence that the person is stupid. People who have such evaluative beliefs about themselves can usually produce an abundance of factual evidence to substantiate their belief. Unfortunately, they often fail to consider that anyone who tries something new is bound to have setbacks, and that people can learn from those setbacks. In the second statement, a descriptive belief stated as a fact is given as "proof" that the person is incompetent. The statement can't qualify as a fact, however, because people can't know in advance that they will fail.

Whether based on facts or descriptive beliefs, negative evaluative beliefs of this kind will almost always inhibit the willingness of people to work up to their potential. People who have such beliefs tend to be depressed, frustrated, and filled with self-pity. As a result, they tend to be passive and to avoid situations in which they may be asked to take initiative (and these are good clues that they don't think too highly of themselves). Since they have condemned themselves with their own beliefs, they are seldom willing to take risks. Needless to say, such people need no enemies, and we can anticipate that they will resist change. Their negativism prevents them from looking forward to anything new. People who have such low self-regard are hard to work with, because their pessimistic outlook casts a cloud over everyone around them. Before their readiness to change can be increased, something will probably have to be done about their inhibiting evaluative beliefs. Perhaps a few victories will help these people see themselves more positively.

The Personnel Transfer Issue

Les Martin was manager of the advertising department in a company that recently experienced reduced sales. To solve this problem, top management decided that some people should be moved from advertising to sales. This seemed like the option because advertising was the most over-staffed department, and the company didn't want to hire people lacking knowledge of its products. Les said that he could transfer three employees to sales without jeopardizing the advertising program. Top management let Les decide which three employees should transfer to sales.

In a meeting, Les asked for three volunteers from his staff of ten to transfer to sales. He said that they had already decided to downsize advertising by three positions, and that he believed all ten could succeed in sales. He offered a one-step salary increase as an incentive for transferring. After hearing this, the meeting was silent, without volunteers. Les expected resistance because advertising enjoyed higher status than sales. However, he thought the salary increase would motivate three people to transfer.

When no one volunteered, he asked to meet with them separately, prepared to justify why they shouldn't be transferred. Following these meetings, Les believed that three employees in particular, Eduardo, Dick, and Carmen, had weak arguments. All three said they wouldn't be good at sales but gave different reasons for their negative evaluative beliefs. Eduardo said he had no prior experience (fact). Dick revealed that he failed at a sales job in another company (fact). Carmen said her personality wasn't forceful enough (evaluative belief).

Instead of transferring these three over their objections, Les developed a strategy to lower their resistance, based on information from these meetings. Since Eduardo's belief was incomplete (he had no evidence),

Les offered to let him develop skills by working part-time in sales and part-time in advertising until he had the confidence necessary to move.

He learned that Dick did fail in a sales job very different from the one in this company. He helped Dick see that he couldn't compare his experience with the present opportunity because the two were dissimilar. Dick said he would try the new job.

Although Carmen believed she wasn't extroverted enough to succeed in sales, she admitted knowing little about the sales jobs in the company. Les arranged for her to spend time with the sales manager and talk with sales personnel. From this, Carmen discovered that the job didn't require a "smooth operator" and was relieved, because this changed her concept of her ability to do the job. She looked forward to being in sales.

By patiently developing and implementing a strategy tailored to specific causes of resistance in each case, Les succeeded in transferring all three to the sales department. If he had not taken time to do this, their new manager would have inherited three employees who didn't want to be there.

It is also possible for people to use evaluative beliefs about others as a way of resisting change. There are two major ways that this happens. The first way is to speak highly of other people so they will get stuck with an assignment ("I think Joe is the best one to do that"). In a situation like this it's important to find out if people genuinely believe Joe would be the best one or if they are trying to pass the buck. Observing what people do and say over time will provide clues that can be used to determine if praise for others is being used as a form of manipulation. People are often duped into doing things others don't want to do because they are so flattered by the praise that they don't see the hidden intent.

The second way is to speak very negatively about others. I'm often puzzled by how quickly people label others as incompetent. People rarely make negative comments openly to another person; such remarks are usually reserved for informal conversations between people discussing someone else who isn't present. Through this process, beliefs about the incompetence of others are spread through the grapevine. The basis of these beliefs is seldom scrutinized—people require very little evidence to pronounce someone incompetent—and the person who is the brunt of this gossip is unable to present the other side. This is unfortunate and potentially damaging because such beliefs are bound to inhibit the relationship between those who hold the belief and the "incompetent" person. The person is judged guilty before the defense can present its case.

Of course, people can develop negative evaluations of others that relate to issues besides competence. Sometimes they stem from lack of respect that develops from previous experience or misunderstandings. At other times they might come from prejudicial attitudes or from envy, jealousy, or competitiveness ("He doesn't deserve that job"). Then there are times when people simply don't like each other for reasons that they can't adequately define ("There's just something about him").

Frequently when differences between people are identified and resolved, the negative evaluative beliefs dissolve; at other times, however, people stubbornly maintain their views even though there's no real justification for them. We should do whatever is possible to bring the reasons for such beliefs to the surface. We may not be able to get people to like each other, but we can insist that they cooperate in order to meet job requirements.

Negative evaluative beliefs about the organization can also cause resistance to change ("This is the worst organization I've ever worked for"). It's important to identify and deal with conditions giving rise to such beliefs. A thorough analysis is necessary, because sometimes negative statements make the organization a scapegoat for beliefs about self or others. Gathering additional evidence will help you uncover the actual beliefs and the reasons for them.

Here's a list of typical statements and questions. Heard any of these?

Evaluative Beliefs About Self

"I'm terrible when it comes to dealing with other people."

"I'm incapable of putting my thoughts in writing."

"I'm about as inept at this as anybody could be."

"Let's face it, I'm just a screw-up."

"Why should anybody listen to me?"

"I must have been a fool to think I could do that."

"I'm smarter than all of them put together."

"If you look up the word incompetent, you'll see a picture of me."

Evaluative Beliefs About Others

"He's the most qualified. Let's give him the job."

"Steve has the personality necessary to handle such a delicate matter."

"Mary, I got tied up on some other assignments. Could you handle this for me? You're better at this sort of thing than I am anyway."

"What do you expect from a product of affirmative action?"

"That's the worse thing he could have done."

"I don't think he has enough on the ball to handle that."

"That's like putting the wolf in charge of the hen house."

"He's friendly enough, but . . ."

Evaluative Beliefs About the Organization

"This is a lousy place to work."

"This job stinks."

"We have the worst management structure I've ever seen."

"The pay and benefits here are terrible."

"The training offered here is a complete waste of time."

"It was the best job I could find at the time."

"Here we go again."

Predictive Beliefs

Whereas descriptive beliefs are interpretations about what's true or false, and evaluative beliefs are interpretations about what's good or bad, *predictive beliefs* are interpretations about what's going to happen in the future. Predictive beliefs allow people to project themselves ahead and to ask "What if . . .?" This question can take people down a number of different roads. First, "What if . . .?" can be used proactively to brainstorm ideas and explore possibilities. This is how visions for new and better ways of doing things are created. Second, "What if . . .?" can be used defensively to examine the implications of *not* doing something. Remember that people are still vulnerable to having bad things happen whether they act or don't act. Sometimes there's greater risk in not acting than in acting. Therefore, it can be very useful to pursue the question, "What if we don't do this?"

Performance Evaluation Procedures Under Attack

Pete Moreno, manager of data processing, had six first-line supervisors reporting directly to him. During the past five years, complaints filed against these supervisors increased. Not sure why this was happening, Pete met with representative employees in the department asking for suggestions. They recommended more employee involvement in routine performance evaluations of supervisors. Thinking that this was a good idea, he and the company's organizational development specialist designed an instrument for rating supervisors on job-related dimensions.

Although this procedure could be useful in identifying correctable deficiencies and reducing grievances, the six supervisors resisted it. They said that it would undermine their authority and give unhappy employees opportunity to vent hostility at them (predictive beliefs). Pete explained that the instrument would be a learning tool, and that he could recognize unfounded criticism. The supervisors still opposed the idea. Pete promised to consider the matter further and discuss it with them again at a future meeting.

Pete suggested that the reasons stated for opposition were not the only ones. He was fairly certain that the supervisors feared that critical comments by employees on the instrument might put their jobs in jeopardy, that the evaluation results would harm them rather than help them.

After considering alternatives, he focused his strategy on one supervisor who was on probation because of employee complaints. Pete offered this supervisor the option of using the instrument to measure his progress during the probationary period. The supervisor agreed, since he had been making a real effort to improve his performance. When the evaluation came back, Pete and the supervisor discovered deficiencies the supervisor was unaware of. From this information, they jointly planned ways to correct these deficiencies. Within three months, the supervisor improved and was removed from probation. This particular supervisor, previously against the method, now spoke highly of it. Other supervisors agreed to try it. After experience with the method, anxiety about job security evaporated, and evaluations became routine. Grievances were reduced, and the relationship between supervisors and employees improved.

Finally, "What if . . .?" can be used to estimate the degree of risk associated with a particular decision. Although this activity is necessary to prevent ill-advised decisions, people are capable of either minimizing or exaggerating risk. Those in the former category are vulnerable to acting when they shouldn't, making impulsive or irrational decisions. In contrast, those in the latter category are vulnerable to not acting when they should. People resisting change tend to dwell on the worst-case scenario, constantly asking, "What if this happens?" and "What if that happens?" Psychologist Albert Ellis refers to this behavior as "catastrophizing." Anyone trying to reason with people who see gloom and doom around every corner knows how frustrating this can be. After listening to even the most logical and compelling presentation, they still have room for one more, "Yes, but what if . . ."

The effectiveness of people's predictive beliefs largely depends upon the quality of the facts and/or descriptive beliefs upon which they're based. Accurate facts and empirically based descriptive beliefs are more likely to result in viable predictive beliefs than inaccurate facts and non-empirically based descriptive beliefs. The purpose of market research, feasibility studies, and contingency plans is to help improve the "hit rate" of predictive beliefs.

It's crucial to understand how predictive beliefs work, because they're almost always involved in cases of resistance. If you propose change and people raise objections based on facts, descriptive beliefs, and evaluative beliefs, you can usually get them to state a predictive belief by asking, "What do you think will happen if we make this change?" It's very important to do this, because predictive beliefs that foresee danger trigger a great deal of fear, which then has a negative impact on the change process.

In the discussion on descriptive beliefs, I described the deductive, inductive, and cause-effect fallacies. One more fallacy I will discuss pertains to predictive beliefs—the predictive fallacy. A *predictive fallacy* occurs when someone concludes incorrectly that since something was true in the past or is true in the present, then it will be true in the future. People are capable of formulating predictive fallacies relating to self, other people, and the organization.

There are two common predictive fallacies concerning self. The first one occurs when people predict that they will fail at something, even though they've never had any experience with it. When presented with a challenge they say something like, "Oh, I could never do that." If you ask for a reason, they may say that since they didn't succeed at such and such, they won't succeed at this either. In my experience this kind of thinking can often be traced back to negative descriptive and evaluative beliefs about self that produce fear of failure.

Similarly, when people's initial efforts to do something are less than successful, they may develop a predictive belief that they will be unable to succeed at this in the future. This belief is shown in such statements as, "I've never been very good at that, and I don't think I ever will be," or "I tried that once and it didn't work out; I don't see any point in trying again." The most damaging thing about statements like these is that a belief regarding past performance is used to conclude that future efforts will also fail. But how can someone know what will happen in the future? The words "I will fail" make failure sound preordained, as if there's no way to change it. Although stated as a fact, this is a predictive fallacy. When you hear people make statements like these to resist change, challenge them to reveal their "evidence." Ask them to prove to you that they won't be able to do it, but then assist them in envisioning more positive outcomes—to see themselves doing it. After some successful experiences, the "I will fail" attitude often disappears, and new opportunities may open up for the person.

Also be aware that people don't like to admit that they are afraid of failure or that they have negative beliefs about their abilities. If you observe them closely enough, however, such beliefs will usually show up in what they say or do. For example, if people have a pattern of escaping or avoiding situations, inhibiting predictive beliefs may well be involved.

The predictive fallacy can also come into play concerning people's beliefs about others. These beliefs frequently take the form of negative prediction about what others can and can't do. Examples are "He could never learn to do that" and "She would have a difficult time getting used to our tight production schedules." When this happens, try to get at the person's rationale for such predictions. Asking such questions as "Can you tell me more about why you feel the way you do?" can be quite helpful in distinguishing between accurate and inaccurate beliefs.

Finally, the predictive fallacy can influence people's predictive beliefs about the organization. For example, take the statement, "We tried that is the past. It didn't work then and it won't work now." This is the motto of many people who resist change. To begin with, the facts and descriptive beliefs pertaining to the past or present may be inaccurate or incomplete. Even if they are accurate, this doesn't necessarily mean that something will or won't happen in the future. When proposing change, therefore, doing your homework in advance will pay off when a predictive fallacy surfaces.

Here are some other predictive beliefs focusing on oneself, other people, and the organization.

Predictive Beliefs About Self

"I would never be able to do that."

"I couldn't handle moving to another department."

"The added responsibility would be too much for me."

"There's no reason why I can't do it."

"Oh, I'll get an offer."

"I've never felt so sure of anything in my life."

"I can't lose."

"Whatever I do, you can count on it to be wrong."

"If I failed, it would be terrible."

Predictive Beliefs About Others

"He'll never change."

"If you tell her, she might hold it against you."

"I can always tell how he's going to react."

"You can never tell what he'll do next."

"Our employees will never go along with that."

"I'm sure he won't mind."

"Just watch, he'll mess it up."

"He couldn't learn that if his life depended on it."

"You can do anything you want if you put your mind to it."

"You just watch; he'll react the same way he always does."

Predictive Beliefs About the Organization

"That idea will never fly in this organization."

"If you want to get ahead, you'll have to go somewhere else."

"With our track record, we better not chance it."

"I know this will work if we just give it a chance."

"It's a sure thing."

"If they can do it, why can't we?"

"This product is going to be a real winner."

"Come on, that's not going to happen."

"It's time for a bold move."

"You're new here aren't you? Well, that won't work here."

Values

So far we've talked about facts and three different types of beliefs: descriptive, evaluative, and predictive. Values are also a type of belief, representing people's views about what's important in life. They are in a separate category from other beliefs. While descriptive, evaluative, and predictive beliefs have to do with the mind, or thinking, values concern the will, or deciding. Values represent people's criteria for making decisions. They play an executive or gatekeeping function in the motivational cycle. To use an analogy, if the personality were an organization, facts and beliefs (descriptive, evaluative, and predictive) would be the employees, and values would be the CEO. The employees (facts and beliefs) have input, but the CEO (values) makes the final decision. The CEO usually accepts employee recommendations, but can also choose to ignore their suggestions or even do something inconsistent with them.

The reason for this is that facts and beliefs *may* affect choice, but values *must* affect choice to qualify as values. Here's another way of stating this: facts and beliefs define a moment; values define a life. It simply doesn't make sense to say that something is important to you and then not do anything about it. One or more values are either openly stated or implied in everything people do. Earlier I made a distinction between genuine values, which actually guide a person's choices, and bogus values, which are affirmed verbally but not acted upon. Both types of values can be involved in resistance to change: people can resist because it goes against their actual values, or they can resist because they want people to think it goes against their values.

Another factor affecting resistance is the intensity with which people hold their values. We hear about people ready to die or kill for such values as freedom, religious tolerance, the right to own land, and so on.

There are people just as passionate about such workplace values as affirmative action, inclusiveness, diversity, gender equity, and empowerment. I indicated in Chapter 3 that a value and its opposite exist along a continuum of relative importance (e.g., security versus risk taking). Someone who believes that a change threatens a deeply cherished value ("They're trying to take away our dignity!") will likely show more resistance than someone who places a lower priority on that value ("I don't like the way they treat us either, but let's be realistic about this—you can't beat the pay and benefits"). Understanding such differences among people will help you anticipate their reaction to impending change.

Distinguishing between a value and a belief during a verbal exchange can be quite tricky, but the ability to discern such differences is crucial to understanding and dealing with resistance. The following statements illustrate how to spot values when someone speaks:

▲ Statement 1: "I've been offered a job in the shipping department" (fact). "It probably would help my career if I made the move" (predictive belief), "but I feel a sense of loyalty to the people I'm working with now" (value). In this example, the person is resisting change because loyalty is more important than career advancement.

▲ Statement 2: "I know I was wrong to say what I did in front of the others" (evaluative belief), "but he's tearing down what it's taken us years to build up" (descriptive belief). "I had to do something to protect our interests (value)." In this example, the person uses a value for protection to justify doing something he/she believes is wrong.

▲ Statement 3: "I've spent a lot of time thinking about this and I just can't go along with the change" (fact). "There are too many factors that haven't been taken into consideration" (descriptive belief) "and, in the long run, I think it will hurt the company" (predictive belief). "I also think they're doing it in a very devious way" (evaluative belief). In this example, the person advances a number of beliefs to resist change, but the value(s) remain unstated. The value can often be drawn out by asking a question to get at what the person thinks is important. If you asked, "What do you think is the most important consideration here?" the person might say, "They have to be honest and aboveboard with us or we'll never be able to trust them." This allows you to see that the change process is violating the person's value for honesty.

The Unassertive Employee

Mark Andrews, the only black person in marketing, was one of five assistant managers in the marketing department headed by Sara Jackson, who was white. After six months on the job, Mark continued to be very quiet and unassertive. He rarely made suggestions during staff meetings and seemed to accept what others thought best. This troubled Sara because the main function of marketing was to create new methods for selling products.

Sara tried to find out why Mark seemed to resist participation. In conversations with Mark and other employees, she postulated that Mark was quiet because he believed white employees were prejudiced. From this hypothesis, Sara developed a strategy she felt would be effective. She separately asked the five assistant managers to encourage Mark to feel that he belonged. During the next few months everyone encouraged Mark, but he remained quiet and unassertive.

Sara was puzzled by Mark's unchanged behavior. In reviewing the problem, she discovered from Mark's personnel file that, although he had considerable management experience, his background in marketing was limited. This additional evidence helped her form a new hypothesis: Mark's behavior stemmed from inexperience in marketing. During a routine evaluation with Mark, she mentioned concern about his reserved team participation and asked if he felt prepared for the job. Mark admitted that he lacked experience, but said he was quiet during meetings because he believed it was important to listen to other's ideas (value).

Sara agreed with him that it was important to listen but stated that he should also contribute ideas of his own. Mark said that he would work on this. Within a short time, Mark began participating more in meetings and became more outgoing in asking others for help. He also attended several marketing training programs, which stimulated his thinking. In time his contributions became increasingly insightful. The importance he had placed on listening had blocked his effectiveness in his new job; his emerging value for expressing his own ideas ultimately made him a vital team member.

Since values are subjective choices, it's impossible to prove that they are either right or wrong. Nevertheless, we can still examine them in terms of their consequences. Using this as our criteria, some values will be more viable or useful than others. Here are some more statements showing that values are being used to resist change. As you read each statement, think about how you might respond.

Values About Self (Personal Values)

"I don't want to change. I'm perfectly content to stay the way I am now."

"It's not important to me to have more authority."

"That's not on my list of priorities."

"Some people enjoy power and prestige, but I see these as meaningless goals for myself."

"That may be important to you, but it isn't to me."

"The salary is less important to me than opportunities for advancement."

"Frankly, my dear, I don't give a . . ."

Values About Others (Social Values)

"It's important that we're honest with each other."

"Let someone else help her; I'm just not interested."

"What you think really doesn't matter to me."

"Working with them is something I'd rather not do."

"You can do whatever you like."

"He doesn't care about . . ."

Values About the Organization (Organizational Values)

"Our mission should be . . ."

"What we need to emphasize is . . ."

"In the future, I see the organization . . ."

"We should be devoting more energy to . . ."

"We need to shift our priority to . . ."

"The organization doesn't care about . . ."

"Who cares what the goals are? I just do my job."

The Resistance Identification Exercise

To gain some experience in distinguishing facts, beliefs, and values, complete the Resistance Identification Exercise below. You'll find the answers on the next page (no peeking).

Read each statement below and indicate in the space to the right whether it reflects a fact, descriptive belief, evaluative belief, predictive belief, or value. The answers are on the next page.

1. "Some of the changes they're making are unethical." _____
2. "I don't know how to operate a computer." _____
3. "That will never work in this organization." _____
4. "We should place more emphasis on customer success." _____
5. "I don't think they're telling us the real reason for this change." _____
6. "I just want to be treated fairly." _____
7. "These cutbacks will ruin us in the long run." _____
8. "Diversity is his hot button, not mine." _____
9. "In this company it's who you know that counts." _____
10. "The only way we can protect our jobs is to never go home." _____
11. "Everyone affected by the change should be involved." _____
12. "If you say what you think, you'll probably be the first to go." _____
13. "It isn't right for them to keep us in the dark this way." _____
14. "The newspaper says more layoffs are expected." _____
15. "They don't care what happens to us." _____
16. "They say that, but they really don't mean it." _____
17. "They're going about this all wrong." _____
18. "I never received the training they promised me." _____
19. "I bet they go back to the old system within six months." _____
20. "I want a win-win out of this." _____

Answers to Resistance Identification Exercise:

1. Evaluative belief
2. Fact
3. Predictive belief
4. Value
5. Descriptive belief
6. Value
7. Predictive belief
8. Value
9. Descriptive belief
10. Descriptive belief
11. Value
12. Descriptive belief
13. Evaluative belief
14. Fact
15. Descriptive belief
16. Evaluative belief
17. Descriptive belief
18. Fact
19. Predictive belief
20. Value

Diagnosing Causes
of Resistance

In Chapter 7, I provided guidelines for identifying specific facts, beliefs, and values that may be causing resistance. Although it's possible for resistance to stem from a single fact, belief, feeling, or value, this would be an exceptional situation. There is also the possibility that you might be identifying a symptom rather than the cause of resistance. Therefore, when you are trying to initiate change, don't accept people's statements at face value because they may not be the cause of resistance. The cause may well be related to facts, beliefs, and values that aren't explicitly stated. In separating symptoms from causes, your catalog of people's facts, beliefs, and values can be especially useful. It can help you consider a specific statement in conjunction with other things you've observed a person say or do.

Of course, it's impossible to become aware of all of a person's facts, beliefs and values, and it isn't necessary to do this when encountering resistance. In any situation certain of these variables will be more relevant than others. Facts, beliefs, and values tend to form patterns, and as you attempt to put a specific statement into perspective, you'll need to identify other relevant facts, beliefs, and values in that pattern. The work you did in building your catalog will pay off here. Without this effort, your assessment will be based on incomplete information, and the problem may continue despite attempts at solutions.

Consider the statement "Cross-functional teams are a complete waste of time." This is an evaluative belief explicitly stated. However, it could be tied directly to unstated facts, beliefs, and values, such as: "Sam Jones told me that they tried using cross-functional teams at X corporation and concluded that it was a complete failure." (While it's a fact that Sam Jones said this, the statement may only reflect an evaluative belief that Sam holds.) "I don't think our employees would put up with a more demanding system of accountability" (predictive belief). "In fact, I think it could actually hurt our efforts to encourage more employee involvement in decision making, particularly at the lower levels" (value). You can see that these variables are all relevant and need to be identified in order to adequately deal with the resistance.

In the example above, it's possible that the predictive belief is the core cause of resistance. If you dealt only with the stated fact and value, therefore, it is unlikely that the resistance would dissipate. In contrast to many real-life situations, this example is fairly uncomplicated. In actual practice, it isn't necessary to belabor efforts to identify a "core" fact, belief, or value. Most people don't have the time to do this, and frequently it will be difficult and maybe even impossible to get to the core because key variables never surface. People usually aren't that open about what they think. Also, in most cases you are dealing with teams, not with individuals, and each person will have a unique pattern. Try to uncover as many variables as possible without becoming bogged down in the process. You probably will be able to gain enough information to make a significant impact on the resistance.

You should also be aware that there are many reasons people speak out as they resist change. Sometimes people deliberately mention a fact, belief, or value to disguise the real reason for their resistance. In the example above, the value may have been presented in a calculated move to keep the person's fear of losing control hidden. At other times, people may sincerely hold a stated fact, belief, or value and be unaware of the connection between this and unstated facts, beliefs, and values. In either case, it's a good idea to gather as much information as possible about the unstated variables because it may be necessary to deal with them before the resistance can be lowered. The most effective way to do this is to ask non-threatening questions relevant to the specific situation. Some examples of possible questions are given below. Questions about feelings are included because they can be useful in getting at facts, beliefs, and values.

Facts

"What information are you basing that on?"

"How do you know that's true?"

"What evidence do you have?"

"How did you arrive at that conclusion?"

"What facts do you have to back that up?"

Beliefs

"What's your opinion of this change?"

"Do you think this change will work? Why not?"

"What problems do you see with this change?"

"Why else don't you think we should make this change?"

"What do you think is going to happen?"

"Can you think of ways that we could make this change easier on employees?"

"Do you see any alternatives to this change that might be better?"

"How can I help you implement this change?"

Feelings

"How does that make you feel?"

"What are your concerns about this?"

"I can see you're upset. Can we talk about it?"

"You sound angry. Can we discuss the situation?"

"I sense frustration in your tone of voice."

"It looks like something's bothering you. Do you want to tell me about it?"

Values

"What's important to you about how this is handled?"

"What outcomes do you want to see from this change?"

"What's the bottom line for you?"

"How would you prefer that we deal with this?"

"What criteria do you think we should use to evaluate alternatives?"

"Do you see anything positive that could happen if we change this?

"What are your priorities?"

So far I've been talking about resistance indicated by something a person says. Sometimes, however, people will listen attentively as you announce a change without expressing any opposition, at least verbally, but fail to implement it. This silent resistance is frequently an effective way to get you to abandon the change. Obviously, the primary clue that the change is being resisted is that nothing happens. There are times when this form of passive resistance represents a conspiracy to foil the change ("Don't pay any attention to him. He'll forget about it in a few days"), while at other times it may be due, for instance, to a lack of adequate instructions ("I'm not sure what he wants us to do, but I'm afraid to ask him"). To determine why the change has not been implemented, however, it's important to follow up by asking questions about the progress being made or about any difficulties that are getting in the way of the change effort. This verbal interaction should help identify whether or not the problem stems from resistance.

Common Causes

Although I've tried to make it clear that there many possible causes of resistance, in my experience eight reasons stand out as being the most common. Originally, I came up with six causes, which I described in my article "Scaling the Walls of Resistance" in the October 1995 issue of *Training and Development.* Later I realized that all of the causes had to do with beliefs and none of them focused on values, so I added the seventh cause. Then several colleagues convinced me that lack of trust was an additional reason for resistance, so I added that to my list. I may discover more common causes, but these eight represent my thinking at this point. The Change Opinion Survey, presented in Chapter 1, is designed to help you discover if one or more of these eight common causes are responsible for resistance to a specific change.

Following are the eight common causes. In Chapters 9 and 10, I offer some potential solutions for each cause.

1. They Believe Their Needs Are Being Met Already (Descriptive Belief)

In other words, they have no incentive or motivation to change, because they're content with the way things are now—if it's not broken, don't fix it. As long as this is true, change will be viewed only as unnecessary or negative.

My colleague Mike Morris told me about the time he started working with client organizations going through paradigm shifts related to the global economy. He said he would get very excited about what he was learning in these organizations, but when he returned to his office he had trouble getting some of his staff to understand what he was talking about. Mike said this was very frustrating, because while he knew that globalization would transform his consulting firm, the employees seemed comfortable with business as usual. Mike was at a point where he needed leadership from everyone, while others were content to let him continue leading. Feeling trapped by the gap between what he needed from his staff and what they needed, he decided to "blow up" his company by transforming it into a more virtual organization.

2. They Believe the Change Will Make It Harder for Them to Meet Their Needs (Predictive Belief)

They see the change as a threat instead of something that could be helpful. In situations like these, facts tend to be less significant than the beliefs (assumptions, conclusions, and predictions) stemming from them. For example, when managers talk about making the work more "efficient," employees often interpret this to mean that they will be doing more work. If a change is presented as making the work easier, employees worry about positions being eliminated. Their concerns will need to be addressed to gain support for change. It's normal for people to be concerned about how they're going to be affected by change, but unviable, pessimistic beliefs about bad things happening are damaging, because they are often based on inaccurate, incomplete, or mistaken information. These beliefs lead to fear and to reliance on values that emphasize protecting oneself against the perceived threat.

This is why people resist learning new technological skills. Protesting that it makes their work harder rather than easier, they continue using older equipment or software until they are in danger of losing their jobs. For many of these people, claiming that new technology will make their work harder is only an excuse to cover up their fear of learning new skills.

3. They Believe the Risks Outweigh the Benefits (Predictive Belief)

As I indicated in Chapter 4, some people err on the side of seeing too little risk with change, while others err on the side of seeing too much risk. Both perspectives can be challenging to deal with. We have seen that change isn't inherently good, and resistance isn't inherently bad. For people to resist negative or harmful change is healthy. Our focus, however, is on situations in which people believe the change is harmful when this isn't actually true. As long as they believe the risks outweigh the benefits, they'll be afraid of the change and try to defend themselves against it. It's important to help them explore what they consider to be the risks, otherwise fear will prevent them from considering the benefits.

4. They Believe Change Is Unnecessary to Avoid or Escape a Harmful Situation (Predictive Belief)

Some examples of harmful situations are bankruptcy, a hostile takeover, and a decline in market share, profit, revenue, productivity, quality, morale, or competitive position. Many changes being introduced in American organizations now are responses to increased competition from other countries. Leaders maintain these changes are necessary to survive, but many employees don't believe this, since they can't literally see the competition. They may believe the changes are just another way to get more work out of them. These employees are in denial. It's important for them to face reality or be left behind.

5. They Believe the Change Process Was Handled Improperly (Evaluative Belief)

People are capable of resisting not only the change itself, but also the methods used to bring it about. This can happen if they didn't have any input into the decision, they don't like how the change was introduced, the change was a surprise, the timing of the change was bad, or they feel manipulated and deceived by management. People react to these with anger, because the methods used go against their values and violate their need for respect. We live in an age when employees expect to have their views considered and to be treated with dignity. People should be asked for input if

they will be affected by the change

you need their commitment to implement the change

they have information or ideas to contribute

they expect to be involved

they could learn from the experience

you want to expand or strengthen your base of support

6. They Believe the Change Will Fail (Predictive Belief)

People can resist change because they don't have confidence it will work, or they don't believe the resources are available to implement the change successfully. The anxiety stemming from these concerns will make it more difficult for people to support the change effort.

Sometimes when people are afraid that they won't be able to adjust to a change, they cover up fear by insisting that the change won't work. You can usually tell there's an underlying issue, because they argue against the change regardless of what you say. In such cases, you must look beneath the surface to get at the real issue and deal with their resistance.

7. The Change Is Inconsistent with Their Values

Since values represent people's beliefs about what's important, they will resist change that is inconsistent with their standards or priorities. Gaining support for new or different priorities is one of the greatest challenges of attempting to lead others through change.

In Chapter 4, I compared the values in the past with those needed for success in today's organizations. I've known many managers who have had trouble embracing values for teamwork, networking, and interdependence, because they equate this with giving up control. Only when they learn that work will still be done by other people, even though there isn't a direct reporting relationship, do they become more receptive to these new values.

8. They Believe Those Responsible for the Change Can't Be Trusted (Descriptive Belief)

People will resist change if they believe that leadership either doesn't have their best interests at heart or isn't being open and honest with them about the change and its impact. If people have trouble trusting each other during routine times, they will trust each other even less during times of change. Mistrust puts people in a defensive posture, causing them to focus on the risks of change. It also causes them to focus on protecting themselves instead of cooperating with others.

The New System for Monitoring Expenditures

Marie Shepard, manager of purchasing and supply, annually submitted budget estimates for the next year's supplies. Because she underestimated expenditures for the last two months of a previous budget, she exceeded the budget by 10 percent. Extra funds were taken from another department's budget, and people in accounting took time from other responsibilities to straighten this out. Because of this problem, Marie's supervisor asked her to devise a better way of keeping track of expenditures, so that she would not run short again.

Marie reviewed systems for monitoring expenditures and selected the one that proved most successful in companies similar to hers. She developed procedures to implement the new system and introduced it at a weekly staff meeting. Although Marie was excited about the system, the staff didn't share her enthusiasm. They expressed considerable resistance toward the procedures. Most considered the current system the best available (evaluative belief) and felt that there was no need to change it. Several argued that the budget problem wouldn't occur again (predictive belief).

Based on the reports she read, Marie was convinced that the new system had definite advantages over current procedures (descriptive belief). Before it could be successfully implemented, however, she needed to overcome her staff's resistance. In thinking through their reluctance, she could not find any reason for resistance except their preferring the status quo. Therefore, she needed to encourage them to want the new system rather than the old. She recalled that two people showed less resistance than others during the staff meeting, but they went along with the group. So she asked them to implement the system as a pilot test to see if it was more effective. They agreed.

After six months, both employees were enthusiastic about the new system. It helped them keep better track of expenditures while cutting down on paperwork. Other employees gradually became interested in using the new system; their evaluative belief about the old system changed. Marie concluded that she might have been more successful at first if she had involved the staff in selecting a new system. Since she chose it, assuming that its merits would be obvious, their resistance caught her off guard. She needed to reassess matters and find a way to encourage them to adopt the system. The pilot test spared her from ordering implementation of the new system over staff objections.

Since organizational change often is implemented through teams, a high level of trust among team members is crucial for success. In fact, I believe team trust is so important to overcoming resistance to change that I have devoted the next chapter entirely to this subject. Before we get too far ahead of ourselves, however, test your skills in identifying resistance by completing the following Resistance Diagnosis Exercise.

Resistance Diagnosis Exercise

Purpose

The Resistance Diagnosis Exercise is designed to give people some hands-on experience in diagnosing resistance. This exercise is intended to take thirty minutes.

Procedure for Group Use

1. Explain that participants will now have an opportunity to diagnose resistance.

2. Hand out a copy of the Resistance Diagnosis Exercise worksheet to each participant, and give these instructions:

    Think of an example of someone you work with who resists change.

    In the space provided on the worksheet, indicate what the person does and says to show resistance. Try to identify the resistance pattern by categorizing what the person says into facts, beliefs, feelings, and values.

    Then indicate your initial diagnosis, what additional information you need to confirm the diagnosis, and what questions you will ask to gather this information.

3. Give participants fifteen minutes to complete the exercise.

4. Ask participants to share their examples with the whole group.

5. Provide feedback to participants and ask them to give each other feedback.

Procedure for Individual Use

1. Think of an example of someone you work with who resists change.

2. On the Resistance Diagnosis Exercise worksheet, indicate what that person does and says to show resistance. Categorize what he or she says into facts, beliefs, feelings, and values.

3. Specify your initial diagnosis, what additional information you need to confirm the diagnosis, and what questions you will ask to gather this information.

Resistance Diagnosis Exercise

What does the person do?

What does the person say?

Facts

Beliefs

Feelings

Values

What is your initial diagnosis regarding the cause of resistance?

What additional information do you need to confirm the diagnosis?

What questions will you ask to gather this information?

Building Trust

9

Trust is a key factor contributing to productivity, quality, morale, and organizational growth. Mistrust, on the other hand, saps the team of valuable time and energy, contributing to organizational suicide. Trust helps foster readiness to change, whereas mistrust fosters resistance to change.

One of the primary problems with mistrust is that it operates insidiously below the surface, and instead of dealing with it directly, people often build their work around it. With increasing competition, however, the assumption that mistrust can be tolerated is no longer viable. A basis for trust must be established if a team is to have any hope of developing its full potential. This chapter will shed some light on this important topic by discussing the dynamics of trust and mistrust, describing actions leading to mistrust, and offering suggestions for enhancing trust. Following this, I provide some general principles for effective leadership.

The Dynamics of Trust

Trust can be defined as believing another person has your best interests at heart, whereas mistrust is believing that the other person does not. Mistrust is a feeling that the other person is trying to control or manipulate you to their end, rather than sharing control to accomplish some joint end. Trust is a dynamic variable that fluctuates up or down, depending on how we interpret another person's behavior. Thus, it's

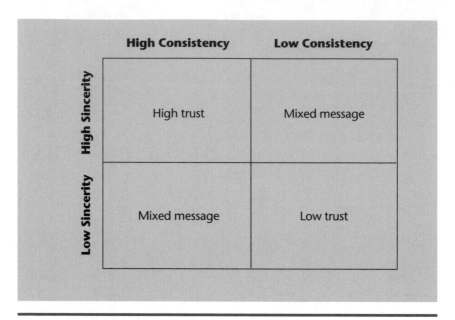

	High Consistency	**Low Consistency**
High Sincerity	High trust	Mixed message
Low Sincerity	Mixed message	Low trust

Figure 9   Inputs for Trust

possible to trust someone to a great extent one minute and less the next. We make adjustments on a conscious or subconscious level all the time as we interact with other people.

Trust is an output that depends on certain inputs. In deciding whether or not to trust someone (the output), we evaluate their behavior according to its consistency and sincerity (the inputs). Consistency has to do with whether or not the other person is ethical, reliable, and dependable. The question we ask ourselves is, "Can I count on this person to do the right thing?" Sincerity has to do with whether or not the other person is genuine and nonmanipulative. The question we ask ourselves is, "Can I count on this person to be really concerned about me?" Consistency focuses on the predictability of the other person's observable behavior, and sincerity focuses on the other person's motives, which can't be directly observed but must be inferred from his or her verbal and nonverbal behavior. As John F. Kennedy said, "Sincerity is always in need of proof."

Trust demands both consistency and sincerity; one without the other won't do. We need to believe the other person not only will do the right thing but will do it for the right reasons. Figure 9 summarizes the effects of high and low levels of consistency and sincerity on trust.

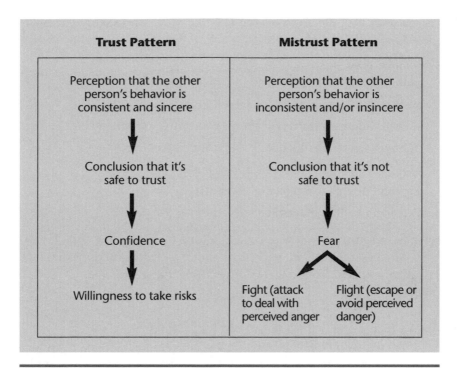

| Trust Pattern | Mistrust Pattern |

Figure 10   Patterns of Trust and Mistrust

The condition of high consistency and high sincerity leads to trust; whereas the condition of low consistency and low sincerity leads to mistrust. The conditions of being consistent and insincere ("He's doing the right thing but doesn't really care about us") and being inconsistent and sincere ("She cares about us but doesn't follow through") send mixed messages that undermine trust.

Trust is a crucial issue because we're aware that other people are capable of hurting us physically, emotionally, and financially. In other words, relationships with other people involve risk, and we're careful not to take risks unless we believe it's safe to do so. Our behavior will vary tremendously depending on whether or not we trust the other person. This is depicted in Figure 10.

When people trust, they are willing to make themselves vulnerable to another person, because they believe it's safe to do so. When they mistrust, people spend their time protecting themselves from a situation they perceive as threatening. When people are in this mode, often they react in ways that cause others to mistrust them, creating a vicious cycle.

Research by Dale Zand, as reported by Golembeiwski in *Renewing Organizations: The Laboratory Approach to Planned Change,* has shown that in organizations in which high trust conditions exist, there is

more open discussion of ideas and feelings

greater clarification of goals and problems

a more thorough search for alternative courses of action

a greater sense of influence by all participants

more satisfaction with problem-solving efforts

a greater desire to implement decisions

a stronger feeling of team cohesiveness

Results were the opposite in organizations in which low trust conditions are present. Thus, it's very important to eliminate actions that lead to mistrust and to replace them with actions that build trust.

Actions Leading to Mistrust

A wide variety of actions can result in mistrust. It occurs, for example, when people

say one thing but do another

make agreements they don't keep

say one thing to one person and something else to another person

pretend to agree with others

try to discredit others

focus on others' mistakes

withhold information

make excuses for mistakes

undercut others

gossip about others

play politics to get what they want

make decisions affecting others without involving them

put each other down

blame others for mistakes

have hidden agendas

compete with each other

try to get even with each other

criticize each other

have a "we-they" mentality

openly attack each other

give more negative feedback than positive

spring surprises on others

ignore input from others

form themselves into camps	try to intimidate each other
seek win-lose outcomes	use information to their own advantage
look out for their own interests	
use manipulative tactics	distort what people say

Once trust has been violated it is difficult to restore because people erect psychological barriers around their relationship with each other to protect themselves from getting hurt. Mistrust will continue indefinitely and become part of the corporate culture unless people are willing to confront trust issues directly, eliminate actions contributing to mistrust, and engage in actions that will foster trust.

Suggestion for Enhancing Trust

Trust can be increased by replacing the negative actions discussed above with more positive actions. Some examples of such actions are as follows.

Listen and convey understanding.

Follow through on agreements.

Resolve disagreements directly and in good faith.

Say what you mean and mean what you say.

Seek win-win outcomes.

Be consistent in what you say to different people.

Honor confidential information.

Give others credit when it's due.

Share information openly.

Take responsibility for mistakes.

Involve others in decisions affecting them.

Avoid actions contributing to mistrust (gossip, blaming, etc.).

Act out of integrity and not expediency.

Steps taken to improve trust will help people become more successful, because energy being wasted fighting each other can be redirected toward more productive pursuits.

Building Trust During Organizational Change[1]

We often discover what works by learning what doesn't work. Over the years, I've seen leaders make many mistakes, some harmless but some devastating. Here are ten general principles of effective leadership that can help you avoid making needless mistakes.

Don't Stray from Your Mission and Vision

The concepts of vision and mission are crucial to leadership during change. A mission defines an organization or team's purpose and is related to *why* we exist. A vision describes a desired future state that would fulfill the mission statement. Sometimes mission and vision are established by a leader, who must then try to gain others' support, and sometimes these aspects of organizational functioning are the products of group interaction and consensus building.

In either case, the mission and vision serve as the context within which people work to develop and implement specific goals and objectives. In Gestalt terms, the former is the forest, while the latter are the trees. As pressure to get results increases, people often lose sight of the forest and become lost in the trees. When this happens, it's important for the leader to remind people of their mission and vision (for example, "Keep in mind what we're trying to accomplish," "Is that consistent with our mission?" "What impact would that have on our mission?" and "What are some other ways we can achieve our vision?").

Don't Tolerate Unacceptable Behavior

While our mission tells us why we exist and our vision defines what we want to become, values and norms describe *how* we plan to work together to achieve these goals. Typically, values and norms evolve over time and remain both unspoken and unwritten unless they are violated. Because some values and norms will be more consistent with the mission and vision, however, it's much better to choose them deliberately. A value for teamwork, for example, is better served by norms stressing listening, open communication, and cooperation than norms emphasizing talking, subtle communication, and competition.

The leader should champion exemplary values and norms and prevent others from appeasing each other by gravitating to the lowest common denominator. The leader's credibility hinges on modeling the values and norms—walking the talk—and holding people accountable for adhering to them. People are quick to spot what they believe to be hypocrisy ("Do as I say, not as I do"), causing them to become cynical about the values and norms. Also, values and norms are meaningless unless positive expressions are rewarded and negative expressions are punished. This serves to make the values and norms *real*. While a leader can't control how others feel about each other, behavioral expectations can be made very clear. People often test the lower limits of behavior to see if the leader is serious about the standards. A leader who insists on positive behavior gains respect, while a leader who ignores negative behavior loses respect.

Behavior is so crucial to a group's success or failure that willingness to abide by agreed-upon values and norms should be a qualification for membership. Making this expectation nonnegotiable sends a strong message ("If you want to work with me, this is what I need from you"). Thus, when people refuse to abide by the expectations, they are deciding not to be in the group. Members allowed to remain in spite of their behavior will undermine team morale and performance—you may win the battle, but you'll lose the war. Once I worked with a group in which one member openly described his contribution as "criticism." While this was stated tongue-in-cheek, his impact on the group was very negative, but since the leader said nothing, the negativity persisted. I found his behavior so irritating that I was relieved when the project was over.

As with mission and vision, people tend to lose sight of values and norms with increased pressure to achieve results. During these times, it's a good practice to remind people of the values and norms. People should be expected to hold each other accountable for their behavior, making this a shared responsibility.

Don't Allow Self-Interest to Prevail over Mutual Interests

Teams or organizations can outperform individuals working alone, but only if members suspend self-interests in favor of mutual interests. Some people have trouble working in teams because they're unwilling to share control; others have trouble because they're unable to make the adjustment from independence to interdependence. In situations like these, self-interest often becomes a barrier to the pursuit of mutual interests. People can sense when someone has a hidden agenda or is seeking personal gain, and the result is resentment, competition, and conflict.

One way a leader can deal with this problem is to make teamwork a criterion for satisfactory performance. If people who promote their own interests aren't held accountable, there's no incentive for them to behave differently. Once they realize that they can't succeed without contributing to others, they're forced to reassess their actions. To remain on the team, some people may have to become more willing to share control, while others may have to develop more effective group skills. For the sake of the mission, the leader should insist on such changes.

Don't Allow Fear to Control Behavior

Fear has a negative impact on people, because the focus is on preventing negative things from happening, rather than making positive things happen. Fear operates as an invisible barrier between people, and the resulting defensiveness and posturing keep them from developing effective working relationships. I've worked with many organizations where the level of fear was so high that people's primary goal was staying out of trouble ("You have to watch out for number one around here"). Fear is so counterproductive that Deming listed *drive out fear* as one of his fourteen management principles.

When people first join an organization their guard is usually up until they see what behaviors are rewarded or punished. If they test the waters and get their hand slapped, it will be a long time before they try it again. This is another reason why norms are so important to an organization. An astute leader can help neutralize the impact of fear and help people meet their needs for respect and acceptance by championing such norms as these:

▲ We will honor confidentiality. Unless otherwise agreed, whatever we discuss will remain within the group.
▲ We will encourage risk taking and honest communication.
▲ We will share our opinions openly.
▲ We agree to disagree without taking it personally.
▲ We will treat each other with respect.
▲ We will deal with issues face-to-face, not go behind people's backs.
▲ Once a decision is made we will support it, even if we don't agree with it.
▲ What we say to team members will match what we say to others.

Don't Allow Subgroups to Control Group Dynamics

Cliques or subgroups are troublesome because they prevent people from becoming a cohesive unit. Cliques tend to compete with each other, promoting self-interest over mutual interests. In addition, the criteria for inclusion in cliques usually work against the organization's mission. I once worked with a group bitterly divided into two camps. One camp was composed of older managers striving to preserve traditional approaches, and the other was made up of younger managers eager to implement new ideas. The older camp viewed the younger one as not valuing its experience, while the younger camp viewed the older one as resisting change. After I worked with the two camps to build mutual respect and find common ground, the group was able to achieve a greater degree of cohesiveness.

The expectation that everyone will work together in a spirit of cooperation needs to be communicated very clearly by the leader, and this expectation should be reflected in the norms. Subgroups will not go away on their own. If subgroups exist or begin to develop, therefore, the leader should indicate that identifying and resolving their differences is nonnegotiable. Sometimes the services of an outside consultant are necessary to expedite this process.

Don't Shy Away from Conflict

All organizations go through three stages of development, which I call "The Three C's:" Courtesy, Conflict, and Cohesiveness. During the first stage, people are polite and diplomatic with each other, as fear inhibits open expression. In the second stage, anger, frustration, and resentment break through the fear, as issues dividing people begin to surface. Anger is a more productive emotion than fear, because it can serve as a catalyst for positive energy. Conflict tends to occur when people disagree about goals and/or methods or when they believe they're being treated unfairly or with disrespect. The latter is usually harder to deal with, because the issues tend to be more personal. In the third stage, people bind together as a result of effective conflict resolution.

A leader shouldn't be afraid of conflict, because cohesiveness can't emerge without it. It's essential for people to learn that they can handle conflict; otherwise they never fully trust each other. Instead of avoiding conflict, emphasize resolving or managing it in a way that increases people's effectiveness. Sometimes it's better for everyone to discuss an issue; at other times it's better for those most directly involved to discuss it privately. Either way there should be norms specifying how to handle conflict, and people should be expected to abide by these norms.

Once I worked with a group in which two members refused to speak to each other. One felt so strongly about it that he said, "I couldn't work with him without compromising my integrity." I offered to facilitate a meeting, and after some pressure from their supervisor, they both reluctantly agreed to participate. I administered the *Myers-Briggs Type Indicator*® to help them understand themselves more fully. Once they learned that their ways of responding stemmed from some basic personality differences, they stopped personalizing each other's behavior and began working through their issues.

Don't Accept Lack of Trust as an Excuse

Mistrust leads to fear and defensiveness, which function as an invisible barrier between people. On the surface it can appear as though people are getting along fine, when in reality their relationships are very calculated and controlled. I've worked with organizations in which mistrust was an unspoken norm, creating an atmosphere of paranoia and suspicion. In these situations, people often use mistrust as an excuse for not dealing with each other and even as a justification for being manipulative ("If you're honest with her, she'll hold it against you"). Obviously, these behaviors will greatly interfere with an organization's effectiveness.

Once activated, mistrust remains as a permanent fixture unless a determined effort is made to get rid of it. Like fear, mistrust must be driven out. To this end, it's important for the leader to remind people of their mission and values and to use the methods discussed earlier in this chapter. Also, since people almost always view themselves as being trustworthy, the leader should challenge their assumptions that others can't be trusted. When trust issues develop, the leader should insist that people face them head-on, and never accept mistrust as a reason for lack of cooperation.

Don't Allow People to Play It Safe

In workshops, people are almost always more open with each other than they were previously, and they regard this as a positive experience. Even if the group establishes a norm for risk taking and people vow to continue their newfound openness, however, after the workshop they gradually revert back to old ways of interacting. Typically, this happens because people get caught up in the demands of work, and since it's safer to be less open, they take the path of least resistance. It's also safer for people to tell you what they think you want to hear than to say what they really think. To maintain higher levels of openness, the leader must both model risk taking and reward those who take risks. These efforts will be well worth it, however, when the organization sustains a more authentic level of interaction.

Don't Be Stingy with Information

Since the sharing of information is such an integral part of team functioning, it's risky for a leader to make assumptions about what people need to know. If people believe that the leader doesn't share enough information, they may conclude falsely that it's being withheld deliberately (descriptive belief), resulting in mistrust and skepticism ("I wonder why she didn't tell us about that"). The sharing of relevant information should be high on any list of team norms. As a rule of thumb, and using discretion, it's usually safer to share too much than too little.

Don't Neglect Process in the Rush to Get Results

When under time pressure (as most organizations are), people tend to forget the norms and use methods they think will get faster results. To prevent this, the leader should remind people of their norms and stress the importance of abiding by them. In addition, it's a good practice to include a review of team process as a standing agenda item at the end of each meeting. Stepping back from content to focus on process gives people an opportunity to self-correct. The leader can frame this discussion by asking such questions as, "How do you think we did today as a team?" "What did you like about the meeting?" and "What could we have done to make the meeting more effective?"

In addition, leaders should specifically ask for feedback about their performance during the meeting. Sometimes people have issues with the leader's behavior, but fear of reprisal keeps them from being honest, unless the leader actively seeks input and follows through by making appropriate changes.

Observing these principles consistently will help you provide your organization with effective leadership and build a climate characterized by trust and mutual respect, which will serve you well when you want to implement change. To apply the principles presented in this chapter to groups you're working with, consider using the Trust Scale and the Plan for Building Trust on the following pages.

Trust Scale

Purpose

The materials in this section allow you to work with your team on building trust, which usually takes from four to eight hours, depending on the amount of interpersonal conflict existing in a team. In some cases, additional sessions will be required.

Specifically you can use the materials to (1) assess the current level of trust, (2) identify behaviors causing mistrust, and (3) develop a plan of action for building trust. The Trust Scale can be administered before and after the workshop to evaluate its effectiveness. Avoid using both the Psychological Need Fulfillment Inventory (see Chapter 2) and the Trust Scale with the same group of people because there's an overlap of items. If you're trying to choose between the two, keep in mind that the former is more comprehensive, while the latter is specifically targeted to the issue of team trust.

Procedure for the Trust Scale

1. Give a copy of the Trust Scale to people.
2. Ask them to complete it anonymously and return it to you on a specified date.

Calculating Scores

The Trust Scale consists of thirty items describing behaviors contributing to mistrust. When you receive all the completed instruments, follow these steps to calculate scores:

1. Add the scores for all team members together.
2. Divide the total score by the number of respondents to get the mean score.
3. Mark the mean score on the Trust Profile.
4. Make photocopies and an overhead transparency of the completed profile.
5. Identify the five to ten items receiving the lowest scores. Place these items in rank order (lowest-ranked item first) on a sheet labeled "Behaviors Most Contributing to Mistrust" and make photocopies.

Using the Results

After reviewing some of the key points about trust and mistrust presented in this chapter, do the following:

1. Hand out a copy of the completed Trust Profile to each person while displaying the overhead transparency you prepared.
2. Explain how to interpret the results:

   The lower the score, the more mistrust exists. Scores from 0 to 60 indicate that mistrust is an issue. The lower your score **below** 60, the more likely it is that mistrust is preventing the organization from achieving its objectives and causing resistance to change.
3. Ask for and respond to questions.

The people on my team

1. Say one thing but do another	4	3	2	1	0
2. Make agreements they don't keep	4	3	2	1	0
3. Say one thing to one person and something else to another person	4	3	2	1	0
4. Pretend to agree with others	4	3	2	1	0
5. Try to discredit others	4	3	2	1	0
6. Focus on others' mistakes	4	3	2	1	0
7. Withhold information	4	3	2	1	0
8. Make excuses for mistakes	4	3	2	1	0
9. Undercut others	4	3	2	1	0
10. Gossip about others	4	3	2	1	0
11. Play politics to get what they want	4	3	2	1	0
12. Form themselves into camps	4	3	2	1	0
13. Seek win-lose outcomes	4	3	2	1	0
14. Look out for their own interests	4	3	2	1	0
15. Use manipulative tactics	4	3	2	1	0
16. Make decisions affecting others without involving them	4	3	2	1	0
17. Put each other down	4	3	2	1	0
18. Blame others for mistakes	4	3	2	1	0
19. Have hidden agendas	4	3	2	1	0
20. Compete with each other	4	3	2	1	0
21. Try to get even with each other	4	3	2	1	0
22. Criticize each other	4	3	2	1	0
23. Have a "we-they" mentality	4	3	2	1	0
24. Openly attack each other	4	3	2	1	0
25. Give more negative feedback than positive	4	3	2	1	0
26. Spring surprises on others	4	3	2	1	0
27. Ignore input from others	4	3	2	1	0
28. Try to intimidate each other	4	3	2	1	0
29. Use information to their own advantage	4	3	2	1	0
30. Distort what people say	4	3	2	1	0

TOTAL SCORE: _____

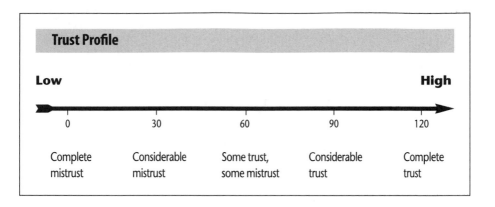

Building Trust

Procedure for the Plan for Building Trust

After you have discussed the Trust Scale, it's time to focus on solutions, by helping people develop a Plan for Building Trust.

1. Explain the purpose of developing an action plan:

   This is an opportunity to pull together information gathered from the Trust Scale and the discussion of behaviors causing mistrust to decide what actions you can take to build trust and eliminate mistrust.

2. Hand out a copy of the two-page Plan for Building Trust to each person.

3. Give instructions for completing the Plan for Building Trust:

   Individually, take about fifteen minutes to identify what you can do to make it easier for others to trust you, and list these ideas in the first box. Please be specific about what you will do and when.

   Then meet with your team to discuss what you can do to improve trust (1) within the team, (2) with other teams, (3) with upper management, and (4) with others (customers, suppliers, distributors, the union, employees, etc.). Use the remainder of the first page and the second page to jot down notes from your discussion.

4. Facilitate this discussion, listing the agreements for action on a flip chart.

5. Ask for a volunteer who will agree to have the flip charts typed and distributed to each person.

6. Ask people to agree on a method for following up on the agreements made for building trust.

7. Summarize key outcomes from this workshop and compliment people for their hard work.

Plan for Building Trust

What I can do to make it easier for others to trust me

What   When

What we can do to improve trust within our team

What   When

What we can do to improve trust with other teams

What   When

What we can do to improve trust with upper management

What   When

What we can do to improve trust with others
(customers, suppliers, distributors, the union, employees, etc.)

Who	What	When

10

Strategies for Overcoming Resistance

Recall that John Kotter describes the main function of leadership as bringing about constructive change, which is achieved by developing a vision, aligning people to that vision, and then motivating them to move toward the fulfillment of that vision. Shared beliefs and values are necessary to fulfill a vision. Taking action to gain support for change is proactive, while dealing with resistance to change is reactive. Regardless of how proactive a leader may be, however, avoiding all resistance to change is an unrealistic goal. In this chapter I present some characteristics of effective strategies for overcoming resistance to change and the resistance strategy model. These principles will allow you to prevent resistance whenever possible and to minimize it whenever necessary.

General Characteristics of Strategies for Overcoming Resistance

There are several general characteristics of most effective strategies. They may sound simplistic or even trite—you may form that evaluative belief. Nonetheless, most of them are present in real organizations where change occurs, and they have powerful results. They're included here to refresh your memory on what works and what doesn't.

Establish a Positive Climate

The beliefs that people have about you and the organization under normal circumstances will affect their responses during times of change. People will begin developing a set of facts and beliefs about you and the organization from the very moment they are employed. If these facts and beliefs are basically positive, they will be more likely to aid efforts during change. If, however, the facts and beliefs are negative, they could be instrumental in establishing a climate of resistance, which tends to interfere with any efforts to initiate change. If you want people to support you during times of change, you need to establish the groundwork for this by demonstrating to them under routine conditions that you are a fair and reasonable person who has their best interests at heart.

Encourage an Interest in Improvement

The chances of successfully initiating change will be greater if you have established conditions under which people want to do their best. If people don't have values for developing themselves or making things better, they will have less incentive to change. A "why bother" attitude may surface, which works against change. On the other hand, if you have helped people cultivate an interest in improving their abilities and performance—a process that in itself requires change—they will tend to be more supportive of other types of changes you initiate. Thus, you can expect the general level of readiness to be greater if previous changes have been personally rewarding and, therefore, positively reinforced.

Show People How Overcoming Resistance to Change Can Help Them

Readiness to change will tend to be greater if you can convince people that a change will leave them better off than they are right now. Sometimes this is very difficult to do. You may have to implement a decision made higher in the organization that will have a negative effect on some or all employees. When that is the case, be honest about it; otherwise you'll lose your credibility.

It is psychologically safer for people to stay the way they are than to risk the uncertainty brought about by something new. Frequently, people would rather stay with the known than venture into the unknown, even if the known keeps them from developing their potential. When change is proposed, people see the possibility for improvement, but they also see the possibility for disaster. It is normal and adaptive for people to weigh the pros and cons of any change before making it. Therefore, if you want to prepare the way for change, lower uncertainty as much as possible by showing people how the change can benefit them.

Help People Increase Their Competence

You are likely to be successful at overcoming resistance to change if the change will provide people with opportunities to increase their knowledge and skills through real accomplishments. A belief in one's competence—-self-confidence-must be based on actual achievements to be real. Any change can increase or decrease the beliefs people have about their competence. Since competence is a personal need that people try to fulfill, they will be less resistant to change if they view it as an opportunity to become more competent. In addition, people who firmly believe in their competence can be expected to be more receptive to change than people who question their competence.

Involve People in Decisions

Generally, people have a more difficult time adjusting to changes initiated by others than by themselves because they have less control over the processes involved, and it is more difficult for them to anticipate how the changes might affect them. When you begin to initiate change, remember that people's first consideration will be focused on how the change will affect them personally. Whether they support or resist change will depend greatly on their beliefs about how the change will affect them.

It is common knowledge that people will be more supportive of change if they are involved in the decision making. The issue here is determining who the change belongs to. If you make the decision without involving those who will be affected by it, the change belongs to you. If the change isn't successful, therefore, the failure also belongs to you. If you involve those who will be affected in decision making, the change belongs to everyone. People will more readily commit themselves to changes that belong to them, and since they have a stake in the results, they will be more motivated to insure that the change is a success.

Cultivate a Value for Teamwork

There is a higher probability that people will work in harmony to implement change if the organization is structured so that they need each other to carry out their various job responsibilities. When people need each other to accomplish work assignments, it is easier for them to develop values for cooperation, teamwork, negotiation, compromise, mutual interests, and so on. These values will be helpful to you in bringing about any kind of change that requires people to work together toward a common goal. This, of course, includes almost any kind of change you can think of. Demonstrate through what you do and say, therefore, that you place a high value on the willingness of people to cooperate.

Don't React Emotionally

One of the most common pitfalls when encountering resistance is to become angry, frustrated, impatient, or exasperated. This type of emotional response is understandable but counterproductive, since it tends to intensify resistance. It may actually give people more reasons to show resistance than they had in the first place. Remember that anger directed toward others is likely to make them afraid or angry in return, which tends to decrease their readiness to change. This could create a pattern in which you encounter initial resistance, which is followed by hostility, which is followed by more resistance. Needless to say, this is a self-defeating cycle that you should try to avoid.

In dealing with resistance, it's more effective to be objective and descriptive than judgmental and critical. Put your emotions to one side, and look at resistance as a challenge rather than a nuisance. This will help you keep your focus on the factors causing resistance, rather than on your reaction to it. When people resist change, it helps to remember that they're trying to meet their needs the best way they know how. Your job is to show them a better way to meet their needs. My brother-in-law, Ron Fradenburg, brought this home to me when he said, "Unless I perceive that you can somehow affect my ability to satisfy my needs, you can't influence my behavior."

Avoid Inadvertent Mistakes

Sometimes people can be their own worst enemy by doing or saying something that inadvertently intensifies resistance. Avoid, for example, offering advice or making a decision before gaining a full understanding of a problem, proceeding without checking to see if others concur with your assessment, criticizing someone in front of others, and showing insensitivity to other's feelings. Avoid making these types of statements:

"In spite of what you think, the real problem is . . ."

"The real reason you're doing this is . . ."

"Your analysis of the situation is totally wrong. The facts you should be considering are . . ."

"I had a problem like that myself once myself, and what you should do is . . ."

"This situation may seem difficult to you, but actually it's quite simple."

"This is a very touchy issue. You better let me handle it."

"You'll just have to trust me on this one."

"If you understood all the factors like I do, then you'd support the change."

"What difference does it make how you feel? You're still going to have to make the change."

Another mistake is to use coercion to bring about change. Under some conditions, changes in behavior can be coerced ("You do it this way or you're fired!"), but it is unlikely that the change will persist after the threat has been removed. Since coercion isn't a very effective way to change behavior, it is useless in changing beliefs and values. People may placate you by pretending to agree with your way of thinking or with your preferences, without any change taking place in their minds. Forced change through the use of scare tactics will serve only to drive the resistance underground, where it will manifest itself in less obvious ways, such as sabotage.

It's also a mistake to argue with people about their beliefs and values, especially if they are held with great intensity. Instead, explain to people the kind of thinking and behavior required to support the change, show them how the change relates to their values, and emphasize the benefits of new values.

Concentrate on Factors Within Your Control

In developing a strategy, concentrate your attention on factors over which you can exercise some control. It doesn't do any good to become frustrated because there are aspects of the situation you can't do anything about. Many people use such factors as organizational policies and procedures to excuse themselves from doing something about resistance—they plead helplessness. If you study a situation, however, you will usually find some things you can do to lower resistance. Identify these factors and invest your time and energy in dealing with them.

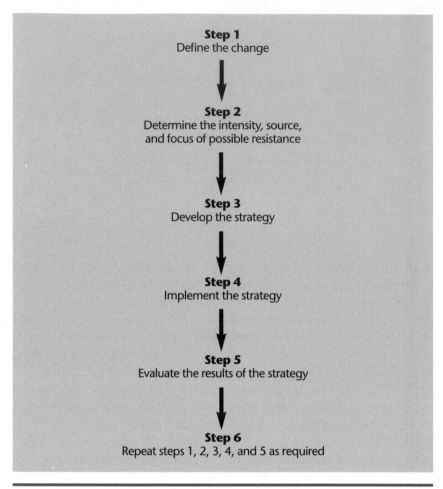

Figure 11   The Resistance Strategy Model

The Resistance Strategy Model

The resistance strategy model (see Figure 11) takes you step by step through a situation in which resistance is either anticipated or has already surfaced. After reviewing the six steps, I hope you believe that your knowledge and skills are more fully developed and that you want to use this approach to overcoming resistance to change. My goal is to convince you of the practical utility of the model and thereby lower any resistance you may have to using it.

Change is inevitable; nothing remains the same whether or not we're aware of it. The question is the role that we play in the process. If others are contemplating change and you're left out of the decision making, your control over the process will be limited or nonexistent. There may be times when you are involved in discussions regarding a change, but you disagree with the decision about what the change will consist of and how it will be implemented.

We are all put in situations where we must carry out changes we don't agree with. Economic considerations, technological advances, the demand for products and services, and other factors may force an organization to make changes that affect everyone. It may be of little consolation that you are involved in discussions regarding these changes. Implementing the inevitable weakens the belief that people have some control over their destiny. Sometimes the most we can do is grin and bear it, hoping that we survive intact.

The resistance strategy model was not designed to deal with change over which you have no control, although information on developing and implementing strategies may be useful in lowering resistance. Rather, the model was designed for proactive situations, that is, situations in which you are actively involved in deciding the nature of the change, how it will take place, and the time frame for implementing it.

Remember, change is necessary for growth and development, for both individuals and organizations. Since change by its very nature entails modifications in how things are currently handled, there are always adjustments as people get used to these modifications. This is true regardless of the magnitude of the change because people must alter their view of reality to make even a small change. And magnitude is a matter of perspective: what seems small to you might be a major trauma to someone else, and vice versa.

The adjustment involved in major changes can sometimes go more smoothly than with small changes. Two people, for example, may show little resistance when asked to switch buildings but tremendous resistance when asked to exchange desks. "It's the small things that'll kill you" suggests the apparent absurdity of situations like this. The mistake here is defining "small" from your own point of view. A good rule of thumb is to look at the meaning of a change from the standpoint of someone who must go through it. Thus, it's a good idea to use the model even when you believe the desired change to be trivial. This will enable you to avoid problems when a change you believe to be small turns out to be large. And if it really is small, using the model won't take much time.

Step One: Define the Change

It's important for you to be as concrete, complete, and precise as possible in delineating what you want to change. Often, people state the desired change in vague or general terms; they describe a direction rather than an end. If the situation does not turn out as they intended, they feel frustrated and think they are encountering resistance when confusion is the only obstacle. Know the concrete outcome you want and state it clearly.

Another common mistake is to define the change only in terms of the *end* result. Most changes involve more than one step. They occur within systems in which the final desired change requires a series of small changes. It is easy for people, in the press of events, to look only at the desired end. If you want to minimize resistance, you must define the intended change as completely as possible. Otherwise, when faced with resistance, you may wrongly conclude that your goal is being resisted when in fact one small step is the source of the problem; and there may be a simple alternative.

Even when you have defined the change as concretely and completely as possible, people occasionally fail to specify the sequence and timing of the change. This can result in a frustrating effort that strengthens resistance.

Step Two: Determine Intensity, Source, and Focus of Possible Resistance

After you define the intended change, determine who will be affected by the change and anticipate how they will respond to it. Ideally, you will be able to predict resistance in advance and take steps to prevent it. Since any change involves adjustment, however, some resistance can usually be expected. If resistance can't be prevented entirely, the next most desirable outcome is to minimize it. The four nonstandardized instruments included in this book, the Change Opinion Survey, Psychological Need Fulfillment Inventory, Megavalue Scale, and Trust Scale can all be helpful in identifying causes of resistance.

Recall that resistance will take different forms depending on its intensity, source, and focus. (See Figure 8, page 110.) The intensity of resistance can vary from little to extreme, and the source can combine facts, beliefs, and values that focus on oneself, others, or the organization. Since any fact, belief, or value can interfere with a person's readiness to change, accurate identification of the intensity, source, and focus of actual or potential resistance is necessary before a strategy can be developed to deal with it. The more evidence you can gather from what people do and say, the better you will be able to separate causes from symptoms and design strategies that deal with causes.

Keep in mind that there is never too much evidence. Since you must infer facts, beliefs, and values from what people do and say, collect as much evidence as possible before making inferences. Always regard your inferences as hypotheses open to modification based on additional evidence. An incorrect inference may be worse than none at all, and your goal is to lower resistance, not to prove that you are right.

Step Three: Develop the Strategy

After you have clearly identified the intensity, source, and focus of actual or potential resistance, develop a strategy to deal with it. A philosophical and moral question becomes relevant at this point: What right do you have to tamper with the beliefs and values of other people? My answer is that we have every right to do this. Sometimes we are irresponsible if we don't do it. The issue is *how* we do it.

Everything you do or say to people has an impact on them in one way or another. There is no such thing as a neutral action. Your effort may be large or small, intended or unintended, but people will be altered in some way every time you have contact with them. Since a change in beliefs or values will leave them better or worse off than before, you have a responsibility to insure that your actions are as constructive as possible.

There is no magic formula for dealing with resistance. Even if your strategy is extremely well thought out, something can always go wrong. Every situation is unique, and human behavior is simply too complex to predict the outcome of any strategy with certainty. In developing strategies, we are limited to thinking of them in terms of the probability that they will be successful. For any instance of resistance, there will always be a number of options. Your job is to thoroughly evaluate the pros and cons of each alternative and select the one with the highest probability of success given all available evidence. Developing a strategy has two aspects: generating specific ideas from the gathered evidence and formulating alternatives from the specific ideas. In earlier chapters I indicated that you can infer people's facts, beliefs, and values by listening to what they say and observing what they do, and provided suggestions for how to do this.

After identifying specific ideas based on your data, formulate as many potential strategies that you can think of. Try to be as creative as possible in developing alternative strategies, so that you don't prematurely rule out an approach that might be effective. You will have time later to assess each potential strategy in terms of its probability of reducing resistance.

Brainstorming with others to generate alternative strategies can often be quite helpful.

The Supervisory Training Controversy

Ed Stewart was director of staff development. Plans for new training programs were approved by a staff development committee, consisting of three company vice presidents. A recent study showed that 90 percent of the new supervisors were promoted from the ranks, and it took about two years before their productivity matched that of experienced supervisors. New supervisors received informal on-the-job training, but Ed felt they could increase production sooner if the company had a structured supervisory training program.

When Ed presented this idea to the staff development committee, one vice president strongly opposed him, saying, "We're obviously not selecting qualified people. A training program would be a waste of money" (first sentence descriptive belief, second sentence evaluative belief). The other two vice presidents were open to the idea and postponed a decision until the next meeting. They asked Ed to provide them with additional justification at that time.

After thinking about the meeting and the vice president's opposition, Ed began considering options. He concluded that it would be difficult to obtain sufficient data to counter the belief that the selection procedure was the main problem. He decided instead to attempt to demonstrate that a training program could provide additional benefits. He knew that the vice president opposing him was reasonable and could be persuaded by logical evidence.

Ed reviewed professional literature dealing with the effects of supervisory training programs on production, as well as turnover rates, grievances, and absenteeism. He also gathered information from companies with similar programs. After summarizing collected data (facts), Ed made a convincing presentation at the next staff development committee meeting. These facts supplemented the "fact" given by the one member, and the committee unanimously authorized the program.

Generally speaking, overcoming resistance is a process of affecting what people think, feel, decide, and do. Thinking has to do with facts and beliefs. Some effective methods for dealing with thinking are to verify facts, clarify beliefs, challenge unviable beliefs, and suggest more viable beliefs.[1] Examples of what you can ask or say to do these things are given in Table 10.

Table 10

Strategies Aimed at Thinking

Verifying Facts	Clarifying Beliefs	Challenging Unviable Beliefs	Suggesting More Viable Beliefs
"What information are you basing that on?"	"What do you think about that?"	"Do your beliefs allow you to meet your needs?"	"A more accurate way of looking at that would be . . ."
"What facts do you have to back that up?"	"What's your opinion?"	"Could these facts be explained in any other way?"	"The facts tend to support the opposite conclusion."
"Do you have all the facts?"	"What do you think is the primary cause?"	"What impact do those beliefs have on your feelings/ priorities/actions?"	"You believe you have no other choice. Let's explore that to see if it's really true."
"Are your facts accurate and complete?"	"If you try that, what do you think will happen?"	"That's not how I see the situation."	"Another way of interpreting that would be . . ."
"How do you know that's true?"	"Do you think that will work? Why/why not?"	"What are the chances of that happening? I think they're quite small."	"This is how I see the situation."
"What additional data do you need?"	"What problems do you see with that?"	"How else could his behavior be interpreted?"	
"What evidence do you have?"	"What do you think he will do?"	"Another way of viewing that would be . . ."	
"How did you arrive at that conclusion?"	"What are the consequences?"	"The facts don't seem to support that conclusion."	
"How can you be sure?"	"What are the risks?"		
"Do you need more information before making a decision?"	"What opportunities do you see?"		
"What are the costs?"	"What alternatives can you think of?"		
	"How can this problem be solved?"		
	"What conclusion have you reached?"		

Table 11

Strategies Aimed at Feelings

Acknowledging Feelings	Clarifying Feelings
"I can see you're upset. Can we talk about it?"	"How does that make you feel?"
"You sound angry. Tell me what happened."	"What are you concerned about?"
"You're feeling frustrated."	"It looks like something's bothering you. Do you want to tell me about it?"
"You're really worried about this."	"What impact do your feelings have on your thoughts/ decisions/ actions?"
"I can feel a lot of tension in this room."	"I know what you think, but I'm not sure how you feel."
"Even though his actions make you angry, you're afraid to say anything."	
"You're discouraged because you haven't been able to make more progress."	

Since feelings are primarily consequences of thinking, they can't be changed through direct intervention. It doesn't do any good to say to someone, "Don't feel that way." Changes in feelings result from changes in facts and beliefs. Nevertheless, when feelings surface, it's important to acknowledge and clarify them. Some ways of doing this are listed in Table 11.

Deciding has to do with values. Some methods for affecting decisions are clarifying values, challenging unviable values, and suggesting more viable values. Examples are presented in Table 12.

Doing has to do with behavior. Some approaches for affecting what people do are to clarify behavior, challenge ineffective behavior, and suggest more effective behavior. Table 13 gives some examples.

First you should always try to do two things: listen and express understanding. Listening is necessary to identify needs and formulate intervention strategies, and expressing understanding is necessary to establish rapport and trust. Until you listen and express understanding, you haven't earned the right to do anything else.

Being heard and understood relates to people's needs for respect and acceptance. Feeling understood allows people to feel less isolated and

Table 12

Strategies Aimed at Deciding

Clarifying Values	Challenging Unviable Values	Suggesting More Viable Values
"What's most important to you?"	"I don't think you can have it both ways."	"One approach would be to place more emphasis on cooperation."
"What outcomes do you want to see from this change?"	"That seems to be less important in organizations now."	"I think creating a greater sense of employee ownership would help morale."
"What's your bottom line?"	"Do your values allow you to meet your needs?"	"Maybe it's time to place a higher priority on gender equity."
"How would you prefer to deal with this?"	"What impact do your values have on your thoughts/feelings/ actions?"	"There would be some real benefits to becoming more customer focused."
"What is your preference?"	"The feedback indicates that a lot of managers don't walk the talk."	
"What factors do you think we ought to consider?"	"Your values seem to clash with those of other team members."	
"What criteria should we use to evaluate alternatives?"		
"Which choice is most consistent with your criteria?"		
"What are your priorities?"		
"What are the benefits?"		
"It sounds like honesty is very important to you."		
"If you had to make a choice, which one would it be?"		
"It looks like you disagree about what's important."		
"What you're saying is you can't remain quiet and still be true to yourself."		
"What would that accomplish?"		
"What purpose would that serve?"		

Table 13

Strategies Aimed at Doing

Clarifying Behavior	Challenging Ineffective Behaviors	Suggesting More Effective Behaviors
"How could you go about doing that?" "What's the first step?" "How could you develop a plan of action?" "Those sound like good ideas. What else could you try?" "What could you say to him?" "Why don't we role-play that?" "After that, what could you do?" "We've talked about how much this situation bothers you. Now let's talk about how you can change it." "How could you go about resolving this conflict?" "You know where you want to go. How can you get there?"	"Do your actions allow you to meet your needs?" "What happened when you did that?" "I'm not sure that will work." "How effective was that?" "I think that would make the situation worse." "I'm not sure that would help you accomplish your goal." "In my experience that tends to put people on the defensive." "It seems to me that would be contrary to your value for . . ."	"Another way of dealing with that would be to . . ." "It might be more effective if you . . ." "Perhaps you could try . . ." "An alternative way of responding would be to say . . ." "One way to build more team cohesiveness would be to . . ." "Perhaps it would help if you expressed more appreciation."

instills in them a sense of hope when discouraged. Unfortunately, people seldom believe that others are willing to listen. It's commonplace to hear them say, "No one listens to me," "No one understands me," or "No one cares what I think about this change." This is why expressing understanding is so important, especially when trying to build support for change. Here are some ways you can express understanding:

"It sounds to me like . . ."

"Let me see if I've got this right."

"Let me summarize what I thought I heard you say."

"I want to make sure I understand. Are you saying . . .?"

"What I'm hearing is . . ."

"So, what you're saying is . . ."

Listening and expressing understanding have value in and of themselves. In fact, sometimes this is all you need to do to gain support for change or to overcome resistance. More commonly, however, these skills are only the launching pad for additional strategies.

A key to managing change is knowing that internal change always precedes external change. That is, change in facts, beliefs, and/or values takes place before change in behavior. Unlike animals, which act on instinct, people engage in mindful change and willful change. Under certain circumstances people can be pressured into changing their behavior, such as when they believe something bad will happen if they don't change, but even then beliefs change before behavior does. Also, once the threat is removed, people will usually revert to the old way of doing things unless the new behavior is supported by appropriate facts, beliefs and values.

In developing potential strategies, keep in mind that strong relationships exist among thinking, feeling, deciding, and doing. If we compared the structure of personality to that of an organization, values would be the executives, facts and beliefs would be the managers, and behavior would be the rank and file. Each is necessary to meet needs, but values assume a leadership role, and facts and beliefs serve as coaches (and sometimes bosses) to behavior. Therefore interventions affecting facts, beliefs, and/or behavior but not values are usually short-lived, which is why so much training, counseling, and consulting fails to produce lasting change.

Change in one area usually changes the others as well. Thus, value change often leads to change in beliefs, feelings, and behavior; belief change often leads to change in values, feelings, and behavior; and so on. Here are some examples:

▲ When people succeed at something they didn't believe they could do, they are challenged to reassess the accuracy of their beliefs.[2] They are also likely to have a feeling of accomplishment and perhaps even to realign values to support the new behavior.

▲ If people are allowed to express their emotions about an upsetting change, they are often able to examine facts, beliefs, and values more objectively. This also can prevent them from making an impulsive decision.

▲ When people are torn between two values (e.g., being honest or being sensitive), ambivalent feelings can interfere with their ability to act. Clarifying which value is more important can help them reduce the ambivalence and move toward resolving the conflict.

Since change in one variable often leads to change in the others, your strategy should start where people are most receptive to change and build from there. Discovering where a person's receptiveness is greatest will require experimentation on your part. It's possible that change in a variable only remotely related to the cause of resistance can lead to changes that have an impact on variables highly significant in causing the resistance.

The Employee Who Feared Promotion

Barbara Hunter, an effective interviewer in the human resources department for three years, had a master's degree in business administration. In discussions with her supervisor, Judy Hall, she indicated strong interest in management. Judy told her that she had the necessary educational background but would need management training to adequately prepare for advancement. The organization offered an intensive training program for those aspiring to management, and since Barbara met criteria for this program, Judy suggested she take it. Judy told her that she would recommend her for the program and provide whatever assistance she needed. Barbara enthusiastically enrolled.

The first training sessions gave an overview of approaches to management, and Barbara felt comfortable. When training shifted to role-play practice exercises, however, Barbara had difficulty. Because she questioned her ability to succeed as a manager (predictive belief), she finished the course but showed no interest in applying for available management positions. When Judy inquired about this, she said that she preferred personnel interviewing to management (bogus value).

Remembering how enthusiastic Barbara was about management, Judy was puzzled about the sudden change. When asked about this, Barbara explained her problems in the course and said she felt inadequate to take on management responsibilities. While her manager argued that she shouldn't form a conclusion based solely on the experience in the course, Barbara was not persuaded. She was convinced that she would fail as a manager and closed it off as a career possibility.

After this discussion, Judy formed a strategy to deal with Barbara's resistance. She knew that initially Barbara was very confident about her potential, although she had no experience to base this on. That's why Judy suggested the management training program. Judy hypothesized that Barbara's untested confidence was shaken during the course, and she jumped to the conclusion that she could never succeed as a manager (predictive fallacy).

Judy decided to gradually provide Barbara with experiences that might alter her negative belief about her management potential. She appointed Barbara to represent her on major committees and delegated office managerial duties to her. Barbara began developing managerial skills, which changed her belief about her potential. Within a year, she grew as enthusiastic about management as before, and her confidence was backed up by solid experience. She was offered a management position in another division, and became one of the most capable managers in the organization. Although Judy regretted losing Barbara, she was pleased to help someone achieve her goals.

Also remember that at any given time a person will be more receptive to change in one area than in others. A common mistake is developing a strategy around a variable that is not receptive to change. It's a waste of time, for example, to try to change a person's value for security if the person staunchly defends that value. Instead, it might be more effective to indicate that after the reorganization people will be expected to engage in more risk-taking behavior.

Another common mistake in dealing with resistance is to fail to modify a strategy as receptiveness to change shifts from one variable to another. The interplay between facts, beliefs, values, and behaviors is dynamic and fluid. People are constantly exposed to new experiences that affect their perceptions. A person may be very receptive one day to change in a belief but the next day resist such change ("At first I thought the change was a good idea, but now I have some doubts"). Therefore, your strategy will have to be flexible. By listening to what people say and observing what they do, you can see how receptiveness to change shifts among facts, beliefs, values, and behaviors, and use this information to make your approach.

To help you become more adept at developing alternative strategies, Table 14 lists some suggestions for dealing with the first seven common causes of resistance discussed in Chapter 8. (The eighth common cause, *they don't believe those responsible for the change can be trusted*, was discussed in Chapter 9.)

Table 14

Strategies for Overcoming the Common Causes of Resistance

1. They Believe Their Needs Are Being Met Already
Explain why the change is necessary.

Indicate how the change will allow them to meet their needs better.

Determine if they're setting their sights too low.

Discover if they're holding back due to fear of losing something.

Appeal to their sense of challenge.

2. They Believe the Change Will Make It Harder for Them to Meet Their Needs
Discover if their facts are accurate and complete.

Determine if their beliefs are based on accurate information.

Provide additional information to correct mistaken or inaccurate beliefs.

Offer more viable interpretations of the facts.

Ask them what positive results they think can come out of the change.

Suggest ways you could make the change easier for them.

Ask how you can help them implement the change.

Ask for suggestions on how to make the change work better.

Ask for alternatives to the change that might be more effective.

Follow through on agreements reached to improve the situation.

3. They Believe the Costs Outweigh the Benefits
Ask them to discuss the costs.

Determine if the costs are based on accurate information.

Provide additional information to correct inaccurate or mistaken beliefs.

Offer more viable interpretations of the facts.

Listen to and respond to their issues and concerns.

Point out how the benefits of the change relate to their values.

Ask them to think of additional benefits.

4. They Believe the Change Is Unnecessary to Avoid or Escape a Negative Situation
Provide facts about the current condition of the organization and the competition.

Explain how the change will help the organization survive and grow.

Listen and respond to their issues and concerns.

Ask for their support in making the change work.

Table 14

Strategies for Overcoming the Common Causes of Resistance (continued)

5. They Believe the Change Process Was Handled Improperly

Ask for and listen to their concerns.

Apologize for mistakes, or the issue will never go away.

Provide additional information (not excuses), as needed.

Ask for suggestions in order to avoid similar situations in the future.

Be honest about suggestions you can and cannot accept, and indicate why.

Follow through on agreements reached to improve the situation.

6. They Believe the Change Will Fail

Ask for and listen to their concerns.

Discover if their facts are accurate and complete.

Determine if their beliefs are based on accurate information.

Provide additional information to correct mistaken or inaccurate beliefs.

Offer more viable interpretations of the facts.

Ask for suggestions to help make the change successful.

Ask for alternatives to the change that might be more effective.

Ask how you can help them implement the change.

Encourage them to visualize positive outcomes.

Follow through on agreements reached to improve the situation.

Ask for their support in making the change work.

Express confidence in their ability to implement the change successfully.

7. They Believe the Change Is Inconsistent with Their Values

Ask them to describe the inconsistencies they see between the change and their values.

Determine if the values are genuine or bogus.

Explore the inconsistencies to determine if they are perceived or real and provide additional information as needed.

When the inconsistencies are real, acknowledge their concerns.

Ask for suggestions on how the problem can be resolved.

When possible, modify the change.

If the change can't be modified, state this honestly and ask for cooperation.

Work toward building common ground.

Point out the benefits of the change.

Ask questions to determine if there are other issues involved, such as anxiety about the change or lack of confidence.

Offer your help and support in implementing the change.

Step Four: Implement the Strategy

In implementing a strategy, the two most important factors are *timing* and *pacing*. Timing has to do with when you implement the strategy. An adequate strategy may intensify resistance simply because it was introduced at the wrong time. Of course, it's no easy task to determine when the best time is; and to complicate matters, it's possible to be either too early or too late. The receptiveness of people to your strategy will be greater at some times than at others, depending upon what else is going on in their lives.

The best way to increase the accuracy of your timing is to know those affected by the change as well as possible and to be familiar with how they respond under varied conditions. If you know, for example, that people just found out they aren't going to receive an expected pay raise, now might not be a good time to deal with their resistance concerning work assignments. There will probably be greater receptiveness to this if you wait until later. In a similar manner, personal, interpersonal, or situational variables either related or unrelated to a proposed change need to be considered in deciding when to implement a strategy. This will increase the probability that your strategy will be successful.

Pacing, which is related to timing, has to do with how much of your strategy to introduce at any given time. Even people receptive to change have limits to how much they can handle within a given time span, since any change involves adjustment. If you push people, you could inadvertently create resistance that wasn't there. This is likely to compound troubles if you are trying to implement a strategy to deal with resistance already present. Don't defeat yourself by going too fast. If people begin to show signs of anxiety, stress, or resentment, this is a clue that you should look at the pace of implementing the strategy. Since individuals will vary in their responses to your strategy, you will need to go slower with some people than with others. During times of change, some people require a great deal of reassurance, while others don't seem to need any at all. If you allow for these individual differences and modify the pace accordingly, the effectiveness of your strategy will be greatly enhanced.

Step Five: Evaluate the Results of Your Strategy

Evaluating the effectiveness of your strategy is important in successfully dealing with resistance. Remember that evaluation is not a one-time procedure that is completed after the strategy has been implemented. Rather, it is an ongoing process that begins from the moment you start implementing your strategy and continues until the resistance is reduced as much as possible. Throughout the implementation phase, what people do and say will tell you whether or not your strategy is working. Sometimes your attempts to deal with resistance will lead to dramatic results that are clearly positive or negative. Often, however, the results will show up in small changes that are difficult to recognize. In their zeal to lower resistance, some people overlook or play down small changes. They may even abandon a good strategy if it doesn't meet with immediate and dramatic success.

You can avoid this mistake by keeping in mind that even small change in beliefs, values, or behavior can be a significant sign that your strategy is working. Since these elements are interrelated, a tiny change can signify the beginning of a process that eventually yields tremendous results. Therefore, notice any positive changes, regardless of magnitude, and nurture them to the fullest.

Step Six: Repeat Steps Two Through Five as Required

Since any strategy is a hypothesis about how to lower resistance, you will not know if it is working until you begin to implement it. Therefore, the results of your ongoing evaluation will tell you if you need to modify your approach. Rarely will you be able to develop and implement a strategy without making adjustments. Be prepared to make mistakes and to deal with them as needed; success usually doesn't reach its destination without passing through failure. Some frequent mistakes are

incorrectly assessing the intensity, source, and focus of resistance

basing your strategy on a symptom rather than a cause of resistance

failing to consider all relevant factors in developing the strategy

implementing a strategy not well suited to the situation

failing to adjust the strategy to account for new information

implementing the strategy at the wrong time or at an unrealistic pace

In addition, your strategy may have consequences you could not have anticipated. The strategy may backfire, causing more problems than you had originally. The cause of resistance may change when you are in the middle of implementing your strategy, or people may confront you with counterstrategies that complicate the entire process. For all these reasons, any time you are faced with a setback or failure, you need to repeat steps two through five as often as necessary to accomplish your objective. The biggest error you can make is to assume your strategy is correct and stick with it in spite of evidence to the contrary. The only way you can beat resistance is to be flexible enough to change your own strategy when it appears that another approach would be more effective.

Plan of Action for Overcoming Resistance to Change

Purpose

This exercise is designed to help participants develop a plan of action for overcoming resistance to organizational change. It is intended to take three hours. Participants should bring to this session any relevant information that will help them plan an organizational change, such as the Current/Desired exercise at the end of Chapter 6.

Procedure for Group Use

1. Hand out a copy of the Change Planning Guide to each participant and give these instructions:

   Think of a change you'd like to make in your organization and develop a plan of action for overcoming resistance to and implementing that change. Start by describing the changes you want to make; indicate the ways people's values, beliefs, and behaviors will need to be different to support your change; identify how you can bring about your change; and finally, indicate what you can do to prevent or minimize resistance.

2. Give participants about thirty minutes to complete the Change Planning Guide individually.

3. Divide participants into groups of four people each.

   Group members should take turns (fifteen minutes each) sharing the information on their Change Planning Guide with the group.

4. Ask individuals to share the information on their Change Planning Guide with the whole group, and provide feedback and suggestions.

5. Allow sixty minutes for this large group discussion.

6. Debrief key learning points with the whole group.

   In what ways has this session better prepared you to lead others through change? What aha's are you taking away?

Procedure for Individual Use

1. Think of a change you'd like to make in your organization.

2. On the Change Planning Guide describe the changes you want to make; indicate the ways people's values, beliefs, and behaviors will need to be different to support your change; identify how you can bring about your change; and finally, indicate what you can do to prevent or minimize resistance.

Change Planning Guide

1. What changes do you want to make?

2. In what ways will people's values, beliefs, and behaviors need to be different to support your change?

3. How can you bring about these changes?

How will you communicate your vision for the change to others?

How will you gain acceptance for the change?

Who will you involve in the change decision and how?

What additional information do you need and how do you plan to get it?

What additional resources (staff, time, money, equipment, etc.) do you need?

What is your implementation plan and timetable?

How will you monitor progress?

4. What kind of resistance do you expect and what can you do to prevent or minimize it?

Adapting to a Changing Health Care Environment

Jon Hultman, DPM, MBA

There is an adage in business that says competition is the mortal enemy of profit. Initially, increased competition slows profit growth by making it difficult to raise prices. Later, as competition increases and businesses begin to lose customers, the response is to lower prices in order to retain existing customers and recapture lost ones. This form of price competition sets in motion a downward spiral that ultimately lowers profit for all businesses in an industry. As profitability declines, companies that are inefficient or that attempt to maintain profitability by lowering quality are the first to be weeded out. Over the long term, the most successful companies are those that are able to adapt to change.

Both lower prices and higher quality are necessary to attract customers in a competitive environment, and efforts to achieve them are what compel a company to restructure. In the absence of such an environment, few businesses would undertake this difficult task. This is true regardless of the industry. Remaining at status quo is never a viable option in a price-competitive market. Staying there serves only to delay the changes that must be made in order to adapt and remain in business.

California was the first state in the United States in which doctors faced the problems associated with competition. With a glut of doctors and a ready supply of large businesses anxious to cut the cost of providing health care to their employees, managed care organizations proliferated. They enrolled millions of patients and then directed them to doctors who were willing to provide fee discounts. Soon all physicians had to either agree to treat patients at a discount or face a decline in patient volume. As competition continued to force prices down, declining profitability created an urgency for physicians to make profound changes and adapt to the new environment.

When I faced a "sudden" 50 percent profit drop in my practice, I knew from my business training that there would be no easy solution. Raising fees was not an option. I would have to implement a major restructuring if I were to successfully lower costs without lowering quality. Fortunately, I felt confident that I could do this. However, I was not prepared for the resistance I encountered from my partners and staff when it came time to translate my "vision" into reality.

Adding a new piece of equipment or moving existing equipment from one location to another is not a change that would typically be thought to generate employee resistance. Indeed very little disruption had occurred in our practice a few years earlier when we had increased the number of computers in the front office to assist our billing personnel. The new equipment did not fundamentally change the way we did business. For this reason, employees adapted quickly, but the change resulted in no measurable improvement. On the other hand, moving just one computer to the back office treatment area proved to be no such simple matter. The placement of computer terminals in our treatment rooms was not merely an addition or a relocation of equipment; it restructured or "reengineered" how work was done and fundamentally changed most of our critical business processes. This change turned the office upside down because it blurred traditional front and back office job descriptions. It interrupted traditional lines of authority, creating insecurity, necessitating retraining, and creating unanticipated employee resistance. In placing information at everyone's fingertips, the doctors were forced to address such issues as trust in employee autonomy.

Before discussing the need for changes in our office with my partners and staff, I analyzed our principal business processes, such as patient scheduling, billing, and medical records. I then attempted to quantify the benefits anticipated from restructuring these processes. As a result of managed care, both patient and paper volume had increased, and the additional rules and procedures had increased the complexity of business processes. I drew a flowchart for each process and examined each for wasted effort and bottlenecks. Within six months I was able to dramatically restructure and integrate these processes on paper and reduce the number of tasks by 90 percent. In addition to identifying unnecessary tasks, I was able to identify major bottlenecks that occurred during peak periods. Bypassing them was accomplished through the strategic use of computer terminals located in treatment rooms, which enabled several processes to be changed from sequential to parallel ones.

Solving problems on paper was the easy part. Implementing the required changes was a different matter. The first problem I faced was convincing my partners that in the midst of a cash-flow crisis, we needed to borrow money, purchase more computers, and convert to a different software—something we had done twice before (and as a result, only succeeded in raising our costs). From my partners' perspective, the decision was one of purchase cost; but for the staff, the decision generated fears that their job descriptions might change dramatically, their current skills might become obsolete, and fewer employees might be necessary as a result—all negative predictive beliefs.

Due to the cost of additional computers and the resistance of employees to my new ideas, we took the path of least resistance and delayed action. We were finally forced to make a decision when our receptionist informed us at the end of a busy day that because of our increased patient volume, she needed help answering the telephone and scheduling patient appointments. She noted that during busy periods when she had difficulty keeping up, people on the phone who were put on hold would hang up, and some patients who were waiting to schedule appointments as they exited the office became annoyed and left without scheduling.

Adding another receptionist was not a viable option for us. We attempted a short-term "fix" by asking other front office staff to assist the receptionist in making appointments during peak phone periods. After a few weeks it became clear that this was not going to help, even though other employees often had slack time during which they could answer the phone. With only one appointment book, others could only help by asking patients to hold and wait for the receptionist to schedule their appointments. Only one appointment could be scheduled at a time, regardless of how many people were answering the phone, because the process was a sequential one. The same problem was occurring with patients exiting the office who needed to make appointments. To make matters worse, as she became busier the receptionist had less and less time to discuss future appointments for returning patients, resulting in some being booked for too much time and others for too little.

One of the processes slated for restructuring was patient scheduling. Instead of scheduling return appointments at the front desk, patients would be scheduled by the back office nurse or doctor from a computer terminal located in the treatment room. I estimated that this would reduce the number of interruptions at the front desk by 80 percent. Appointments would be made by the doctors and the back office staff, who had better knowledge and information as to the requirements of return visits. My partners were now convinced that change was needed.

Placing computer terminals in the treatment rooms turned the office upside-down and changed job descriptions dramatically. Work was going to be done differently. Suddenly, back office employees would be doing "front office work" and doctors would be performing staff duties. Traditional roles and responsibilities would be changed, and employees began to fear that these changes might affect them personally. Fortunately, the only process we were attempting to reengineer at this time was scheduling. Had we attempted to change our billing and accounts receivable processes at the same time (while encountering this resistance), our cash flow might have been adversely affected.

The new scheduling process took four months to implement. Not only did we have to train the doctors and staff to use the new software, but we also had to deal with employees' fears and concerns. Each time a "glitch" occurred in the system, it was seen as "hope" that the process changes would not work and the project would be scrapped. This hope was augmented by the fact that in the early months, scheduling became more problematic and required more time.

After about three months, something exciting began to happen. Employees began to feel more confident in their computer ability, and back office staff began to find that their jobs had become more interesting. Patient flow improved because scheduling was more efficient and appointments were being made for the optimum amount of time. This helped keep the office running on schedule, which was a hit with patients. With 80 percent fewer interruptions at the front desk, the receptionist had more time to spend on the phone with new patients. Not only did this give a better initial impression of the office, but it also allowed her sufficient time to understand the nature of patients' problems and thereby book the appropriate amount of time for them. And even though she spent time discussing treatment with new patients, the receptionist still had slack time to help in other areas as needed, including the back office.

The initial negative predictive beliefs held by employees began to disappear with the success of this new scheduling process. The office environment changed from one of fear to one of enthusiasm. This initial success also set the stage for accelerating the implementation of the remaining reengineering projects. Restructuring the billing processes had the greatest potential for resistance because its establishment was expected to eliminate one job. Under the new process, billing information would be entered directly into computers located in the treatment rooms rather than through the old process of having patients fill out forms, accumulating them in batches, and then storing them for later data entry. Eliminating this duplication of tasks would also eliminate the need for data entry, a job that involved work that was repetitive, boring, and wasteful. The data entry process also actually delayed the billing process and resulted in a lower collection ratio. I felt that the new process could create the opportunity to use this staff person's time for more interesting and productive work and would increase the collection ratio at the same time. Fortunately, this turned out to be the case.

Looking back at our change process, we can see that what started as a survival mission converted our office into a better place to work and a better place for patients to be treated. The disruptions that occurred during the change process were not well tolerated by every employee. I am sure I could have done a better job of preparing employees for the change and helping them adapt. While no one was actually laid off during the change process, due to "natural attrition" we had 40 percent fewer employees by the time we were finished. We have not yet had a need to replace any of the staff members who left, and those who made it through the change process report increased job satisfaction. They are performing more interesting and more productive work, and they have been empowered and given tools that encourage continuous improvement. This streamlined staff is more valuable, and there has been no turnover in the six years since our change.

The transformation we underwent prepared our office to face the future. We can now manage volume increases without hurting quality—and without adding more cost or additional work for the front office. We recognize that we cannot rest on our laurels because the medical marketplace is still in transition. However, rather than fearing change, our staff realize that it can be exciting. Other offices that have attempted to make similar changes have not undergone as smooth a transition. I now realize that what I lacked in human resource skills was compensated for by my enthusiasm and my belief in the vision I had for the practice. While I am able to teach these skills to other doctors through seminars and my book, *Reengineering the Medical Practice,* some doctors have encountered more resistance than I did. One reason for this may lie in the fact that this is my vision rather than theirs; when problems arise their confidence in the ultimate success of the project is often less than mine, making employee resistance harder to overcome. I can see that the issue of managing and dealing with resistance and barriers to change is as important as identifying the changes that need to be made.

Notes

Chapter 1: So You Want to Make Some Changes?
1. Maurer, R. "Resistance wears many faces," *Performance in Practice,* Spring 1998, p. 8.

Chapter 3: The Motivational Cycle
1. The *motivational cycle* should be viewed as a system of complex interrelated processes, not as a linear cause-effect model. For more information on systems thinking, see *The Fifth Discipline* by Peter Senge and *Learning as a Way of Being* by Peter Vaill.
2. Leon Festinger indicated that people are motivated to strive for consistency within their belief system, which can lead to distortion.
3. This formulation is consistent with Albert Ellis's A B C theory of personality, which maintains that A is a fact or event, B is the person's belief about A, which causes C, the emotional reaction.
4. Some writers place values in the affective domain, but consistent with the formulations of such theorists as Milton Rokeach, Albert Ellis, and Aaron Beck, I place them in the cognitive domain. I conceive of values as cognitions that have affective and behavioral consequences.
5. Reprinted with permission from "Today's leaders look to tomorrow," *Fortune,* March 26, 1990, pp. 30–31. © 1990 Time, Inc. All rights reserved.

Chapter 9: Building Trust
1. The material in this section is adapted from my article, "The ten commandments of team leadership," which was published in the February 1998 issue of *Training and Development.*

Chapter 10: Strategies for Overcoming Resistance

1. Albert Ellis refers to challenging unviable beliefs as disputing irrational beliefs.

2. Leon Festinger asserts that when people do something that is inconsistent with their beliefs, they experience "cognitive dissonance." One of the ways they can resolve this dissonance is by changing their beliefs.

Bibliography

Adler, A. (1927) *The practice and theory of individual psychology.* Orlando, FL: Harcourt Brace, 1927.

Badaracco, J. L., and Ellsworth, R. R. (1989). *Leadership and the quest for integrity.* Cambridge, MA: Harvard Business School Press.

Beck, A. (1976) *Cognitive therapy and emotional disorders.* Madison, CT: International Universities Press.

Bem, D. J. (1970). *Beliefs, attitudes, and human affairs.* Pacific Grove, CA: Brooks/Cole.

Bernstein, A. J., & Rozen, S. C. (1994). *Sacred bull.* New York: Wiley.

Blanchard, K. H., and Peale, N. V. (1988). *The power of ethical management.* New York: Morrow.

Brunswik, E. (1947). *Systematic and representative design of psychological experiments: With results in physical and social perception.* Berkeley: University of California Press.

Covey, S. R. (1989). *The seven habits of highly effective people.* New York: Simon & Schuster.

Deming, W. E. (1986). *Out of the crisis.* Cambridge, MA: MIT Center For Advanced Engineering Studies.

Deming, W. E. (1993). *The new economics: For industry, government, education.* Cambridge, MA: MIT Center for Advanced Engineering Studies.

Ellis, A. (1973). *Humanistic psychology: The rational-emotive approach.* Julian Press.

Ellis, A., & Dryden, W. (1987). *The practice of rational-emotive therapy.* New York: Stuart.

Festinger, L. (1957). *A theory of cognitive dissonance.* New York: Harper-Collins.

Golembeiwski, R. T. (1972). *Renewing organizations: The laboratory approach to planned change.* Itasca, IL: Peacock.

Herzberg, F. (1966). *Work and the nature of man.* Orlando, FL: Harcourt Brace.

Hultman, K. E. (1976). "Values as defenses," *Personnel and Guidance Journal, 54* (5), 269–271.

Hultman, K. E. (1978). "Preparing employees for upward mobility," *Training and Development Journal, 32* (9), 10–14.

Hultman, K. E. (1979). *The path of least resistance: Preparing employees for change.* Austin, TX: Learning Concepts.

Hultman, K. E. (1980). "Identifying and dealing with resistance to change," *Training and Development Journal, 34* (2), 28–33.

Hultman, K. E. (1981a). "Gaining and keeping management support," *Training and Development Journal, 35* (4), 106–110.

Hultman, K. E. (1981b). "Increasing your leverage with line managers," *Training and Development Journal, 35* (9), 99–105.

Hultman, K. E. (1982). "The trainer as scapegoat," *Training and Development Journal, 36* (7), 44–53.

Hultman, K. E. (1986). "Behavior modeling for results," *Training and Development Journal, 40* (12), 60–63.

Hultman, K. E. (1988). "The psychology of performance management," *Training and Development Journal, 42* (7), 34–39.

Hultman, K. E. (1995). "Scaling the walls of resistance," *Training and Development Journal, 49* (10), 15–18.

Hultman, K. E. (1996a). "Removing barriers to organizational change," in Hultman, J. A., *Reengineering the medical practice.* St. Anthony Publishing.

Hultman, K. E. (1996b). "Trust: A key to team success." In Hultman, J. A., *Reengineering the medical practice.* St. Anthony.

Hultman, K. E. (1998). "The ten commandments of team leadership," *Training and Development Journal, 52* (2), 12–13.

Jastrow, J. (1927). "The animus of psychical research." In Murchison, ed., *The case for and against psychical belief.* Worcester, MA: Clark University Press.

Kotter, J. P. (1988). *The leadership factor.* New York: Free Press.

Kotter, J. P. (1990). *A force for change.* New York: Free Press.

Lewin, K. (1935). *A dynamic theory of personality.* New York: McGraw-Hill.

Madrick, J. (1995). *The end of affluence: The causes and consequences of America's economic dilemma.* New York: Random House.

Maslow, A. (1962). *Toward a psychology of being.* New York: Van Nostrand Reinhold.

Massey, M. (1989). *What you are is where you where when . . . but not what you have to be.* Niles, IL: Nightingale-Conant.

McClelland, D. C. (1975). *Power: The inner experience.* New York: Irvington.

McClelland, D. C., Atkinson, J. W., Clark, R. A., & Lowell, E. L. (1953). *The achievement motive.* Englewood Cliffs, NJ: Appleton-Century-Crofts.

McDougal, W. (1926). *An introduction to social psychology.* John W. Luce.

Rokeach, M. (1968). *Beliefs, attitudes, and values.* San Francisco: Jossey-Bass.

Rokeach, M. (1973). *The nature of human values.* New York: Free Press.

Senge, P. M. (1990). *The fifth discipline.* New York: Doubleday.

Slater, R. (1992). *The new GE: How Jack Welch revived an American institution.* Burr Ridge, IL: Irwin.

Tolman, E. C. (1973). *Purposive behavior in animals and man.* Englewood Cliffs, NJ: Appleton-Century-Crofts.

Vaill, P. E. (1996). *Learning as a way of being.* San Francisco: Jossey-Bass.

Index

Acceptance: need for, 21–22, 26; and
    organizational reality, 77–79
Adler, A., 55
Andrews, M., 134
Arnold, B., 98

Badaracco, J. L., 76
Beck, A., 56, 201
Behavior: aspects of, 15–33; and change,
    60–61; defensive, 16; effective, 80;
    and motivational cycle, 35–50; and
    organizational reality, 79–80; strate-
    gies for, 184; summary on, 28; and
    trust, 156–157
Beliefs: and actions, 103; challenging,
    37; in change, 53–56; facts distinct
    from, 36–37, 111; and feelings, 43;
    learning, 51–52; in motivational
    cycle, 36–42; about organization,
    41–42, 70; and organizational reality,
    67–69; about others, 39–40, 69;
    probes on, 141; about self, 38–39, 68;
    strategies for, 181; types of, 36,
    38–42; value distinct from, 72,
    133–134; viable, 67–70. *See also*
    Descriptive beliefs; Evaluative beliefs;
    Predictive beliefs
Bernstein, A. J., 74
Billing process changes, 199
Blanchard, K. H., 76
Brunswik, E., 55
Building Trust exercise, 166–167

California, health care competition in,
    195–196
Cardwell, J., 101
Cause-effect fallacy, 118
Change: ability to, 96–98; aspects of,
    1–92; backgrounds on, 3–4, 15–18;
    and behavior, 15–33, 60–61; and
    boredom, 52–53; conditions for,
    3–13; context for, 51–53; describing,
    178; dynamics of, 51–63; external
    and internal, 53, 185; facts and
    beliefs in, 53–56; in health care envi-
    ronment, 195–200; as inevitable,
    177; and motivational cycle, 35–50;
    in organizational reality, 65–92;
    overview on, 8; process for, 144–145,
    146–147; reactive and proactive,
    61–63; receptivity to, 186–187; resis-
    tance to, 93–194; summary on, 63;
    support for, 5–7; and trust building,
    156–161; and values, 57–60
Change Opinion Profile, 6, 7, 13
Change Opinion Survey, 6, 9–12, 142,
    178
Change Planning Guide, 193–194
Childs, T., 118
Clemens, S., 117–118
Climate, positive, 172
Competence: beliefs about, 38–39;
    increasing, 173; personal, 18–19,
    74–75; social, 19–20, 75–76
Competition: global, 67; and profit, 195

Computer terminal relocation, 196–199
Conflict, and trust, 159–160
Consistency, and trust, 152–153
Cost/benefit analysis: and beliefs, 42;
    of change, 59–60; strategies for, 188;
    and values, 49
Covey, S. R., 76
Crane, M., 115–116
Culture, organizational, and beliefs, 41
Current and Desired Organizational
    Beliefs, Values, and Behaviors,
    106–108, 192

Deciding: in motivational cycle, 43–49;
    strategies for, 182–183; and
    thinking, 44
Decision making, involvement in, 173
Deductive fallacy, 116–117
Deming, W. E., 77, 158
Descartes, R., 35
Descriptive beliefs: and change, 54–55,
    58; concept of, 36; and evidence,
    116–118; about management, 117;
    in misunderstanding, 115–116;
    about organization, 120, 121; about
    others, 119–120, 121; resistance
    from, 114–121, 143, 146–147; about
    self, 119, 120–121; and vindictive
    employee, 119
Doing: in motivational cycle, 50;
    strategies for, 182, 184–185

Ellis, A., 129, 201, 202
Ellsworth, R. R., 76
Employees, as intellectual capital, 4
Empowerment: and continuous
    improvement, 199; from learning,
    66; and needs, 17
Evaluation, of strategies, 190–191
Evaluative beliefs: and change, 54–55;
    concept of, 36; about organization,
    126, 127; about others, 125–126,
    127; about personnel transfer,
    124–125; resistance from, 122–127,
    140, 144–145, 146; about self,
    123–125, 126; and values, 45

Facts: beliefs distinct from, 36–37, 111;
    in change, 53–56; context of,
    112–113; about organization, 114
    and organizational reality, 66–67;

Facts (continued)
    about others, 113; probes on, 141; on
    resistance, 104–105; resistance from,
    111–114; about self, 113; strategies
    for, 181; and values, 72
Fallacies, and beliefs, 116–118,
    129–131
Fear, and trust, 158
Feelings: and beliefs, 43; in motivational
    cycle, 42–43; and organizational
    reality, 69–71; probes on, 141;
    strategies for, 182; and values, 46, 72
Festinger, L., 201, 202

General Electric, vision statement of,
    49
Genuineness: and organizational reality,
    77–78; of values, 45–46, 49, 132
Golembeiwski, R. T., 154
Gould, M., 58
Grief reaction, and change, 62–63
Group dynamics, and trust, 159

Hall, J., 186–187
Health care environment, change in,
    195–200
Herzberg, F., 18, 19
Holt, C., 58
Honesty, and organizational reality, 77
Hultman, J., 195–200
Hunter, B., 186–187

Implementation, timing and pacing in,
    190
Individuation, and change, 52
Inductive fallacy, 117–118
Information, and trust, 161
Information Age, 66–67
Instincts, values distinct from, 44
Integrity: personal, 20–21, 76–77; social,
    21–22, 77–79
Interests, mutual, 75, 157–158
Interpersonal environment, beliefs
    about, 41

Jackson, S., 134
Jastrow, J., 36
Jenson, B., 3–4, 6–7

Kaubman, H., 117
Kelly, C., 119

Kennedy, J. F., 152
Kotter, J. P., 171

Lewin, K., 55
Listening, strategies for, 182, 184–185
Luboff, J., 119

Madrick, J., 66
Martin, L., 124–125
Maslow, A., 17, 20, 21
Massey, M., 47, 59, 81
Mastery: need for, 18–19, 24; and organizational reality, 74–75
Maurer, R., 201
McClelland, D. C., 18, 21
McDougal, W., 17
Meaning and purpose: facts and beliefs for, 53–54; need for, 19–20, 25; and organizational reality, 75–76
Megavalue Profile, 89
Megavalue Scale, 85–88, 178
Megavalues, and needs, 73–79
Mission and vision, and trust, 156
Mistakes, avoiding, 174–175
Mistrust: actions leading to, 154–155; concept of, 151; as excuse, 160; patterns of, 153
Modification, of strategies, 191
Moreno, P., 128
Morris, M., 143
Motivation: aspects of, 35–50; and beliefs, 36–42; and deciding, 43–49; and doing, 50; and feelings, 42–43; summary on, 50; and thinking, 36–42; and values, 43–49
Myers-Briggs Type Indicator, 160

Needs: concept of, 15–16; hierarchy of, 17; meeting, 24–27; and megavalues, 73–79; and organizational reality, 66, 80; psychological, 18–22; and resistance, 143–144; strategies for, 188; unmet, 22–28

Organization: beliefs about, 41–42, 70; descriptive beliefs about, 120, 121; evaluative beliefs about, 126, 127; facts about, 114; and needs, 15;

Organization *(continued)*
personality of, 185; predictive beliefs about, 130, 131–132; values about, 49, 135
Organizational reality: and acceptance, 77–79; background on, 65–66; and behavior, 79–80; and beliefs, 67–69; change in, 65–92; and facts, 66–67; and feelings, 69–71; and mastery, 74–75; and meaning and purpose, 75–76; and needs, 66, 80; and respect, 76–77; and values, 71–79
Others: accepting, 78–79; beliefs about, 39–40, 69; descriptive beliefs about, 119–120, 121; evaluative beliefs about, 125–126, 127; facts about, 113; predictive beliefs about, 130, 131; resistance in, 102–105; values about, 48, 135

Paradigm shift, in organizational reality, 65–66
Patient scheduling, processes for, 197–199
Peale, N. V., 76
Perfectionism, as barrier, 74–75
Plan of Action for Overcoming Resistance to Change, 192–194
Plan for Personal Change, 90–92
Planning, down-side, 58
Potential, development of, 74, 172
Predictive Belief Continuum, 56
Predictive beliefs: and change, 54–55, 58; concept of, 36; about others, 130, 131; about performance evaluation, 128; resistance from, 127–132, 140, 143–144, 145, 146; about self, 129–130, 131
Predictive fallacy, 129–131
Process: strategies for, 189; and trust, 161
Psychological Need Fulfillment Inventory, 23, 29–33, 162, 178
Purpose. *See* Meaning and purpose
Pursuing: and change, 63; and vulnerability, 17

Readiness: enhancing, 172–173; resistance compared with, 95
Reed, N., 115–116

Resistance: active and passive, 102, 142; analysis of, 93–194; anticipating, 178–179; assessing, 95–108; background on, 95–96; common causes of, 142–147, 187–189; and control, 175, 177; from descriptive beliefs, 114–121, 143, 146–147; diagnosing, 139–149; emotional response to, 174; from evaluative beliefs, 122–127, 140, 144–145, 146; from facts, 111–114; general characteristics of strategies for overcoming, 171–175; and inability to change, 96–98; intensity of, 109, 112, 132–133; locating causes of, 109–137; matrix of, 110; in others, 102–105; overview on, 93–94; patterns of, 139–140; positive and negative, 98–99; from predictive beliefs, 127–132, 140, 143–144, 145, 146; to promotion, 186–187; readiness compared with, 95; reasons for, 95–96, 140; in self, 99–101; strategies for overcoming, 171–194; strategy development for, 179–189; strategy model for, 176–191; to supervisory training, 180; and trust, 146–147, 151–169; and unmet needs, 22–28; from values, 132–135, 140, 145–146
Resistance Diagnosis Exercise, 148–149
Resistance Identification Exercise, 136–137
Respect: need for, 20–21, 27; and organizational reality, 76–77
Riley, B., 115–116
Risk taking: and change, 52, 55–56; and predictive beliefs, 129, 144; and trust, 160–161
Rokeach, M., 45, 46, 201
Rozen, S. C., 74

Self: beliefs about, 38–39, 68; descriptive beliefs about, 119, 120–121; evaluative beliefs about, 123–125, 126; facts about, 113; predictive beliefs about, 129–130, 131; resistance in, 99–101; values about, 47–48, 135
Self-confidence, and anxiety, 70–71
Self-worth: and beliefs, 38; and courage, 52; and honesty, 77; need for, 17
Senge, P. M., 201
Shepard, M., 146–147

Significant emotional events, and change, 59
Sincerity, and trust, 152–153
Smithson, K., 117
Stability, change in balance with, 98–99
Stephenson, J., 58
Stewart, E., 180

Teamwork: trust in, 147; as value, 173–174
Thinking: and deciding, 44; and motivation, 36–42; strategies for, 181
Thomas, S., 57–58
Tolman, E. C., 55
Trust: actions leading to, 155; aspects of, 151–169; and beliefs, 40; building, 156–161; concept of, 151; dynamics of, 151–154; inputs for, 152; and monitoring expenditures, 146–147; patterns of, 153; and resistance, 146–147
Trust Scale, 162–165, 178

Understanding, strategies for, 182, 184–185

Vaill, P. E., 65, 201
Value adding, and competence, 76
Values: and actions, 103–104; beliefs distinct from, 133–134; and change, 57–60; exercises on, 81–92; and feelings, 46, 72; genuine, 45–46, 49, 132; instincts distinct from, 44; learning, 51–52; and motivation, 43–49; and needs, 73–79; negative impact of, 47, 71; about organization, 49, 135; and organizational reality, 71–79; personal, 47–48; probes on, 141–142; resistance from, 132–135, 140, 145–146; about self, 47–48, 135; social, 48; strategies for, 183, 189; teamwork as, 173–174; types of, 47–49; and unassertive employee, 134; viable, 71–72, 79

Welch, J., 49
Will, and values, 46
Willingness, and ability to change, 96–98
Working conditions, beliefs about, 41

Zand, D., 154